THEMES, DREAMS & SEASONS

About the Author

Graham Wade, writer and musician, living on the East Yorkshire coast, studied English at Cambridge University, is a Fellow of Trinity College of Music, London, and was elected a Fellow of the Royal Society of Arts in 1982. He has published over thirty books among them his critically acclaimed biographical studies of the great Spanish composer. Joaquín Rodrigo, and of the guitarists, Andrés Segovia and Julian Bream, as well as works on musical history, and a number of slim volumes of poems.

In 2002 he was awarded the Schotts Gold Medal for his contribution to Rodrigo studies and in 2010 won the David St John Thomas Prize for his first novel *The Fibonacci Confessions*. His second novel, *The Emperor's Barber*, was published in 2017. In 2018 he won the Sunday Times Royal Wedding Poetry Competition for his poem celebrating the marriage of Prince Harry and Meghan Markle.

Graham Wade has written for many newspapers and periodicals including *The Times*, *The Independent*, and *The Guardian*, and is an Advisory Editor and contributor to both the British and American *New Grove Dictionary of Music and Musicians*. In 1999 he was appointed General Editor for a series of paperbacks for the leading American music publisher, Mel Bay Inc., of Missouri.

Themes, Dreams & Seasons, *Poems* 1956–2018, collects together over 250 poems and three short stories spanning over sixty years. The poems are presented thematically covering a wide variety of experiences, topics, reflections, and styles, including the intensities of love and loss, meditations on mythologies, character, destinies, travel, the world of nature, and the tragic momentum of time, old age, and mortality.

Themes, Dreams & Seasons

Poems 1956–2018

GRAHAM WADE

Foreword by John Carrington

THE CHOIR PRESS

Themes, Dreams & Seasons

Published in 2019
by The Choir Press
132 Bristol Road, Gloucester GL1 5SR

ISBN   978-1-78963-032-9

Cover image: Edward Hicks (American, 1780–1849).
Peaceable Kingdom, ca. 1848. Oil on canvas,
support: 23 7/8 x 31 7/8 inches (60.6425 x 80.9625 cm).
Collection Albright-Knox Art Gallery, Buffalo, New York;
James G. Forsyth Fund, 1940 (1940:18).
Image courtesy Albright-Knox Art Gallery.

Cover design by Chandler Design Associates Ltd

Typeset in 12 on 15pt Caslon
by Abstract Graphics

for Sue

Contents

Foreword. . . . .*xix*

Winkie . . . . *xxviii*

Juvenilia (1956–1962)

Sea Scene. 2

Wet Streets 3

Sherry-party. 4

From a Wood in Shropshire. 5

Young Love. 6

Meditations, on Chronos. 7

Days 8

Busker. 9

Seventy-odd 10

Vision 11

Matins 12

Patterns. 13

Kingfisher 14

Lord of the Flies 15

Spider in a Jar. 16

From a City Window 17

Beach-comb. 18

In Whim or Design (1968)

Dale 20

Ode to Daedalus 21

Requiem 24

Eclogue 25

Swaledale, Yorkshire 27

Beach. 28

Pastoral. 29
Dog. 30
Austrian Incident 31

CHILDHOOD

War Baby 34
Girl. 35
Children's Playground. 36
I   Mother 37
II   The Meeting 38
III   Looking and Touching 39
IV   The Return. 40
A Boy and a Dog. 41

MYTHOLOGIES

Ancien Régime 46
Requiem for Orpheus 47
Odysseus 48
Skies 49
Apollo 50
Western. 51
Birthday 52
Judgement. 53
Duet 54
Reflections. 55
Memorial 56

THE SEA

December Ship 58
Lyrical Ballad. 59
Thoughts after a Swim 60
Night Glimmers 61

In Memoriam............................. 62

Ship 63

Sailor's Love Song........................ 64

Suicide Note 65

Song of the Drowning Man 66

Song of the Mariner 67

The Drowned Girl 68

Seascape 69

Sunset.................................... 70

Voyage................................... 71

Walk..................................... 72

Sea Mood 73

Meeting 74

Sea Sleep................................. 75

Wave Watcher........................... 76

Letter 77

Night Sea 78

Sea Night 79

Journey.................................. 80

Flamborough Head....................... 81

Voyage................................... 82

Viking Funeral 83

A Sailor Remembers 84

PLACES AND JOURNEYS

Thoughts in Malta 86

Song of the Spanish Saint 87

Short Story 88

Salvador, Brazil 90

Driving through Valencia, Spain 91

Pearl River in the Rain 92

India..................................... 93

Leningrad. 94
Leaving the Falklands 95
Journey 96
Andalusia 97
Lakeside at Night 98
Mongolian Lamasery 99
Ilmington Village 100
The Long Journey 101
Calcutta 102
Algiers. 103
Goats in the Trees 104
Australia. 107
American Suite 108

CREATURES GREAT AND SMALL

Hedgehog 114
Slugs 115
Frog Boys 116
Warwick 117
Mole 118
Loss. 119
Little Brown Dog. 120
Lion in the Zoo. 121
Wild Flower 122
Poor Tiger. 123
Hawk 124
Bird Garden 125
Frog 126
Stoat 127
Bullocks. 128
Spider 129
Giant 130

Frog in the Grass. 131
Giraffes. 132
Escaped Budgerigar. 133
Daddy-long-legs 135
Poor Bull. 136
Bull. 137
Plovers 139
Bear 140
Bird with a Broken Wing 141
A Camel with a Honey-Coloured Hump . . . 142
Nostalgia. 143

SEASONS AND MONTHS

Spring. 146
Sonnet. 147
April Snow 148
Holderness Spring. 149
May 150
Summer End. 151
Autumn 152
Fall. 153
September End 154
Autumn Trees 155
The Winds of Autumn 156
Autumn Leaves. 157
After the October Storm 158
October 159
Fog 160
Poem for October. 161
The Weaver Hills 162
Ice 163
December 164

Snow. *165*
Winter's End. *166*

Bric-a-brac and Ragbag

Scarecrow *168*
Omens. *169*
Strange *170*
Running. *171*
Hong Kong *172*
Doors *173*
Trapeze. *175*

Time's Reflections

Serving Time *178*
Summertime *179*
Love's Time. *180*
Decisions. *181*
Time's Silence *182*
Tiger Time *183*
Sunt lacrimae rerum *184*
Dusk. *185*
Timing. *186*
Time, Gentlemen, Please. *187*
Visit *189*
Playtime *190*

Characters

Widow *192*
Friday. *193*
The Fight *194*
The Boxer. *195*
First Love. *197*

Slaughter Man 198
The Torturer Goes Home to his Children. . . . 199
Spinster. 200
Teacher 201
Train Journey 202
Wedding 203
Judge. 205
Rider. 207
Gardener. 208
Dancer 209
Book Shop 210

FAIRY TALES

Princess. 212
Woods 213
Song of the Fireflies. 214

DESTINIES

Song of the Hanged Man 216
Salmon 217
War Trilogy 218
In Memoriam. 221
City Dweller. 222

OCCASIONAL POEMS AND ELEGIES

Trumpeter. 224
Remembering 225
Dear Jack 227
Retirement Party 229
Guitarist. 231
Royal Wedding 232
Epithalamion 234

Moments

Remembrance 236
Parting 237
To the Music Lesson 238
Quarrel 239
Patio 240
Garden 241
Round Midnight 242
Words 243
The Dream 244
Roof 245
Riding 246
Letter 247
Evolution 248
River Suite 249
Memento 252
The Look of Love 253
Night 254
Absence 255

Reflections

A Cartel of Poets 258
Lorca 259
The Inward World 260
Poem for Hilary Comeau, artist 261
Retrospective Exhibition 263
Rain 265
Things are Not the Same 266
Books I've Never Read 267
Violin 268
Poetry 269

On the Occasion of Antigoni Goni's
Guitar Recital. *270*
Guitar. *271*
The Grand Piano *273*

HUMOUR OR OTHERWISE

Pride. *276*
Song of the Drunk. *277*
Hitler *278*
Banana Skin. *279*
Girl in a Red Hat. *280*
The Chair. *281*
Good Intentions *282*
Poll Tax *283*
Song *284*
Letter Poem. *285*
Reminiscence. *286*
Nursery Rhyme. *287*

PERFORMANCE POEMS FOR CHILDREN

The Last of the Dinosaurs. *290*
The Beginning *292*
King Canute. *294*
The Plague of Frogs *297*
Daniel and the Lions *300*

SWEET TOOTH (OR TOOTH SUITE)

INFIRMITY

Looking at You *310*
Love *311*

More than Ever *312*

Chest Clinic *313*

Hospital *315*

Final Approach. *316*

Homeward Path *317*

After Her Illness *318*

A Lake Called Panic *319*

AGE

An Apple. *322*

The First White *323*

Song of the Old Man. *324*

Suicide Attempt. *325*

Summer's End. *327*

Old Man's Song. *328*

Do Not Be Fooled *329*

My Eyes are Weaker *330*

Curtain. *331*

THE FINAL CHAPTER AND BEYOND

Biddy *334*

The Passing. *336*

The Scattering. *338*

Anna. *340*

Song of the Very Old Man. *341*

After a Funeral *342*

John *343*

Forethought. *344*

Accept *345*

In Memoriam *346*

Leaves. *347*

In a Crematorium Garden *348*

After She Died *349*
Revelation *350*

THREE SHORT STORIES

Gethsemane. *352*
And. *356*
The Golden Guitar of the
Pharaoh's Daughter. *365*

Acknowledgments *371*

Foreword

Let us begin at the end – with the three short stories which conclude this poetry anthology. There are parallels between the prose and the poems. In *Gethsemane (p.352)*, an evocation of the chill of the evening and of what is to come narrows to Jesus's contemplation of an insect, which prompts philosophical conundrums about what limits there may be to an insect's, or Man's, awareness.

In *The Golden Guitar of the Pharaoh's Daughter (p.365)*, Graham Wade tells the pleasingly teasing tale of his memory of having had dreams about supposed realities that were in fact manufactured illusions. The trusted memories turn out to be half-truths. (And we are even provoked to ponder whether this tale in itself is an autobiographical reality or a fiction.) Such is the labyrinth. And we are drawn to reflect again on the natures of our consciousness and of our knowledge, and the limits of our purchase upon them.

The story *And (p.356)* describes the demise of a fictional Amazon tribe, the Yamuri, and their fascinatingly unique language – there is no word for I, and the very word *And* is of much greater significance than we in our presumed sophistication would normally give it. *And* in this community is a cherished word, opening new worlds, which are maybe imperfectly understood, but are vividly apprehended.

There's a valuable metaphor in these three stories for our attempts at understanding, appreciating what we do and don't understand or know, and in particular there is an echo of how words – words of poetry and words of any language – open new worlds for readers, with words to value, to savour, to revisit with accumulating pleasure – new worlds which indeed may be imperfectly understood, which is the very reason why we are drawn to them, as we are drawn to Graham Wade's poetry. (It's worth remembering, too, that he is also a novelist, most recently in *The Emperor's Barber* and also in his remarkable debut *The Fibonacci Confessions*.)

We find the themes of the stories reflected in the poems. For example, in *Trumpeter (p.224)*:

> *Now we must hold on,*
> *Like children in the dark*
> *To what we know.*

And, at the end of *Teacher (p.201)*:

> *Together we could strive*
> *Into knowledge like crabs*
> *Exploring the sea's edge.*

There is another very good reason why it is appropriate for Graham Wade's prose to join his poetry in this book. As the writer Robert Macfarlane has put it beautifully:

Rhythm in language speaks to the back of the scalp, it's what makes the head tingle if you get it right…it's a form of communication…when I'm writing prose I work on the rhythms.

There's a shared territory here, between poetry and prose, and Graham Wade inhabits that territory. Indeed, there's an interpenetration of music, sound, rhythm and word. Graham Wade's professional scholarship has centred on music, especially the music of the guitar. As you read his poetry, and his prose, you sense a natural finesse that blends rhythm, sound and language. Try reading the poems – and the prose – aloud. The back of the scalp will tingle.

By way of illustration, we may take this paragraph from *"And"* where the young children of the tribe take pleasure in the physical and musical aspects of the learning of their language:

> *The toddlers played with the syllables on the tongue, repeated them, rolled them back and forward like an incantation or a trick of memorising, whispered or shouted, growled or sung, prolonging or shortening each syllable and sound, and subjecting the word to an almost symphonic process of variation. After an hour or two of listening to this I found the voices stuck in memory like a phrase of music infinitely refined, repeated till it became part of the beat of one's own pulse.*

In Graham Wade's poetry, our perceptions of the world about us are sharpened, keenly refreshed. They become part of the beat of our pulse. He has written: '*I'm not at all experimental or progressive. I write what comes and*

hone it afterwards.' An over-modest disclaimer, maybe –
the honing in these poems has arrived instinctively,
and they are doubtless the better for that. They work,
evocatively and powerfully, through the crafting of the
images. Distinctions between prose and verse, or between
observer and observed, or between the poem and its
'meaning', dissolve. In Archibald Macleish's memorable
words, *'a poem should not mean, but be'.*

This anthology tracks an evolution of experience
across a lifetime. We progress, for example, from a
young man negotiating the social awkwardnesses of
Sherry-party (p.4), to the *'bitter-sweet emotions'* of
Retirement Party (p.229). An over-arching image is that
of the voyage: the sea, overseas travels, woods, streets. And
birds and animals abound – sometimes creatures whose
powers are fading, sometimes the natural world and its
inhabitants simply enjoyed in grateful and humorous
encounters, on occasion written especially for children.
Nature is seen afresh - *'swallows in evening dress'*, or a
'thrush ill at ease in its brown shift', in the keenly-observed
Pastoral (p.29). In *Lord of the Flies (p.15)* a dying fly
is viewed from within the unusual perspectives of the fly's
world, while *Little Brown Dog (p.120)* and *Frog (p.126)*
present with affectionate comedy touchingly simple
contacts between human and creature.

We also discover a chronicling of quiet moments and
intensities. Images are rarely simply descriptive, often
evocative, often moving. There are allusions to the ancient
myths; and occasional echoes of Yeats and Hardy. Life
is freshly animated, even in the earliest poems. (Don't
be misled by the title *Juvenilia*, that describes the first

section, into expecting immaturities: there are treasures here.)

Later, in an ever-unfolding variety, we find the light and whimsical wordplay of *Girl in a Red Hat (p.280)*, or *Banana Skin (p.279)*, with both adult and child appeal. (There's the fun, too, of the knockabout rhymes in *Performance Poems for Children*.) Frequently the images are arresting. We wish to absorb them, ponder them, as in *Leaving the Falklands (p.95)*:

> *These waters are sad,*
> *Beautiful as light changing.*

Goats in the Trees (Moroccan Suite), Pots in the Sunlight (p.105) provokes this meditation:

> *Pots squat like pilgrims on the ground*
> *Round mouths open in surprise,*
> *They have no tongues and cannot speak*
> *Which makes them infinitely wise.*

More disturbingly, the hands in the photograph of a dead Middle Eastern soldier are *'as brown as dead hares' War Trilogy (p.218)*.

Swaledale, Yorkshire (p.27) presents hills *'purple with blood'*, and ends with:

> *Desolate birds before the breeze*
> *Above brute rocks*
> *Drift in brisk frieze.*

The richness of the closing word *frieze* lies not only in the beauty of the image, and the satisfying finality of the rhyme, but also in that it gives the whole poem an (almost literal) frame.

In *Dale (p.20)* 'flights of grouse' are 'gunned in the wind's teeth'. The shock of gunned alerts us to a deep recognition that the grouse, in or out of the shooting season, have other battles to fight.

The themes deepen as we 'face the silence beyond'. The section *Times Reflections* e.g. in *Decisions (p.181)* and *Time's Silence (p.182)* considers life's sheer, ungiving momentum, posing decisions and self-examination. The focus tightens on 'the downward slide', the difficulties of finding direction and meaning (as in the world of the Yamuri tribe).

Consider these lines from *Birthday (p.52)*:

> *This birthday is a piece of glass*
> *In the mosaic of my days,*
> *I see no form within the mass,*
> *I read each word but not the phrase.*

Or from *Sunt lacrimae rerum (p.184)*:

> *The top spinning*
> *Till it stops.*

There are sombre responses to dark events, as in *Suicide Attempt (p.325)*. The past and the future darken for *Odysseus (p.48)* – at sea, gazing back at '...*the debris / Of past voyages*', and destined for '...*the coming tide of pain / At the horizon's edge*'. There's a similar image in

In Memoriam… (p.62) – 'We too shall go. / Already we / Almost hear the sea'. The first line of *A Boy and a Dog (p.41)* pulls us up sharp:

I always live as if I'm going to leave quite soon

Sometimes a poem leaves us with a sharp provoking twist, such as *After She Died (p.349)*, *The Torturer Goes Home to his Children (p.199)*, and the close of *Royal Wedding (p.232)*, the poem which won The Sunday Times competition for the best poem about the wedding of Prince Harry and Meghan Markle.

There is a personal history interwoven here too. The four haunting *Mother* poems *(p.37–p.40)* trace Graham Wade's affecting relationship with his birth mother who gave him into adoption, aged three and a half, and whom he meets again when he is aged fifty. *The Passing (p.336)*, and *Biddy (p.334)* centre respectively upon the deaths of his adoptive father and of his adoptive mother. *Parting (p.237)* touches the painful separation from the girl-friend who rejected him in his student years because her parents told her that adopted children had 'bad blood'.

For all this, Graham Wade's is a positive and generous vision. We are enabled through his poems to share a warm and expansive empathy as in *Dusk (p.185)*:

So sleep now
Till turning day brings
Another space,
And morning comes
And the early thrush sings.

In *River Suite, Thoughts (p.250)*:

> *Wine sings a song*
> *Fresh bread tingles the tongue.*

> *Soft light falls on rivers,*
> *Our moon is a poem.*

'*Our moon is a poem*' – our preconception that moon and poem inhabit separate worlds dissolves before us. A poem should not mean, but be.

The final three sections of poems – *Infirmity*, *Age*, and *The Final Chapter and Beyond* – definitively represent Graham Wade's gentle humanity. *Biddy* and *After She Died (p.349)* movingly evoke an ending, and we enjoy the characterful and wry humour with which *Biddy* closes.

Forethought (p.344) crystallises a wistful, plangent beauty:

> *Soon we shall go,*
> *And never see each other.*

> *Love's memory*
> *Will hang in the sunset*
> *Like a spider's web.*

In contrasting mood, *Curtain (p.331)* develops the witty and original construct of the principal characters of *Romeo* and *Juliet* in their seventies – or in some cases in their graves. *The First White (p.323)* muses lightly on an attempt to scissor away the first white hairs. Meanwhile there are poignant and painful descriptions of patients eking out their days in nursing homes (*'damp battlefields of beds'*), and of the scattering of ashes (*The Scattering (p.338)*).

For Graham Wade, in death there are no consolations, but nonetheless we find in these poems the affirming love and tenderness of his regard. Lingering moments are deeply etched.

And it is that crafting of the evanescent vision that is at the core of this lifetime's writing. In *Dog (p.30)* we enjoy the sheer *pleasure* in observation: the dog wittily patterned into an icon, like the birds of *Swaledale*, drifting in their *'brisk frieze'*.

Here, as often elsewhere, Graham Wade offers us fixities that delight – and for a moment – maybe just for a moment – there is stasis amid the endless flux. That indeed is the satisfying paradox that we often find here. Even where the theme is of our irreversible movement towards and beyond the horizon's edge, we have the fleeting consolation and beauty of a *'brisk frieze'*.

Dear Jack (p.227) offers us a keynote:

> *Seeing things we loved, more than before,*
> *Listening to the heart within the voice,*
> *Listening to the pulse within the heart.*

Sentiments that resonate with the heart and pulse of this fine collection.

JOHN CARRINGTON

TAUNTON, NOVEMBER, 2018

Winkie

(for Graham Wade)

Largo, ma non troppo

Mr Wade seldom spoke, even to his stuttering wife, who called my best friend Graham 'W-w-Winkie', and chirped a lot. When he opened the locked door of the small shed of the small garden of his terraced house that backed onto the tracks the screeches sometimes seemed like crazy words. Once we heard 'Churchill's out! Damned war-monger!'

G and I weren't allowed inside, but through the windows, out of sight, we could watch as after work each day he cleaned and restocked the cages of budgies, replacing soiled Daily Mirror with new, adding strands of millet seeds, squeezing cuttlefish bones between the bars, pouring fresh water. Sometimes he let his favourites flip about and perch on him. The place was a bit scary.

Each day he went to work early and came back late after shunting up and down in his black BR 0-6-0 tank not built for curves or speed, shoving mostly empty flats and boxcars, guard's vans and wagons down one siding and up another, bangs and clatters, never accomplishing much that I could see. Beside the cattle-market I'd wave with my Ian Allen trainspotters' book filled with prizes like Mallard, Wildebeest or Blink Bonny, but he never waved back.

One Saturday I went to pick up G to collect fossils from the chalk pits or to fish for sticklebacks while fantasising about Susan Hayward, and, if my parents were out, at my place wrestle until the carpet rolled up and slipped away and we crashed into the china closet bringing down some plates.

This time he motioned me to follow along his dark hallway lined with fragile gas mantles no one ever lit into the front parlour where no one ever went. There (flooded in sun that came through drawn curtains as if they were nothing), was a piano. He sat down and ran his fingers over the keys, absorbed, picking out tunes I didn't know. I slipped out the back, past the quiet birds, and along the track, the long way home.

Soon a guitar sat beside the piano in a case as big as G. Despite his mother's protests, he took to wearing black drainpipes and grew his black hair down to his shoulders. I cut mine short, crew-cut, sported drainpipes too, with winklepickers, and hung out with a rough crowd, or what passed for rough. But still our mothers talked, G's boasting about W-w-Winkie's talents and accomplishments, and mine doing her best with what she had. One day she said 'He's adopted, you know,' as if that was the clincher, and she'd won.

Slowly we lost touch. G left. I left. His father died, then his mother. Then his entire street was torn down.

One autumn afternoon, after a brief visit, I was standing on the platform waiting for my train. Behind me were some wicker baskets just unloaded from a guard's van, each packed with homing pigeons, cooing and shuffling, until a porter opened the trapdoor on top and out they flew, straight up, around, interweaving in and out, sorting out, getting their bearings before all at once heading in the direction they knew, casting no shadow I could see as they shrank into the sky and vanished. I dropped my eyes, and looked along the platform where a train had just pulled in, people getting off, and there, I was sure, was G, all in black, black hair, black guitar case.

I waved, and ran to where he was. He wasn't there. He'd gone.

BRIAN SWANN

PROFESSOR OF HUMANITIES,
COOPER UNION, NEW YORK

Juvenilia (1956–1962)

Sea Scene

(1956)

Waves were growing boys losing
An unsubtle, boisterous poise
Till they became bitter and broke
On the bow's knife-edge.

Where once dancing points of quick-
Silver glass made a lawn of mosaic
Now passion cannot be dispersed.

Until the seabird pirouettes cease,
The fantastic ballet of flying fish
Indulged only beneath the leaping water.

Wet Streets

(1956)

As if suddenly streets assume the status
Of artificial gardens or a stage
Within a wilderness where painted women
Shape foolish gestures across a thousand
Yellow and blood blooms.

Or church-like neon footlights quietly beckoning
Compel the stained-glass pavements to pass their
Quick prismatic illuminations up
To familiar rooms.

Sherry-party

Sugar falls from the tongue
In much the same way as sand
Beats time on time
With a heavy hand.

That hard-pressed saccharin will lose
Its savour yet and to this end
Hope remains distilled within the context
Of a higher power,
Who gazes deeply through small spectacles,
Disinterested,
All at sea inside that blotchy skin.

We continue to perspire and shake off
Limp phrases, like shaking
Stones inside a tin to make a noise.

From a Wood in Shropshire

(1959)

Through the trees the indistinguishable roofs reach
   with a
Red hand for the hills, the land dead to the touch,
Throwing off a little wheat with a careless gesture.

The wood has a matt carpet, poised midway between
Persian exotic and English rustic, somewhat untidy.

Its stagnant moss rich with green velvet
The bark of the trunks brittle with brown,
Through the leaves like mist the smoke lifts
From the haggard town.

The wood withdraws its continence,
Indicates its memories of Roman men
Pacing the green and gold mosaic of its fall,

Or more recently young lovers passing
Dream-like through the leafy hall.

While the grey people flit through the branches,
Hesitant and fugitive, twinkling within
Their forest prison.

Young Love

So you go home to mother
And I'll go home to bed,
To lie awake and ponder
All the silly things I said.

Then when the rosy-fingers
Come probing through the dawn,
As an old dream lies and lingers
New doubts will be still-born.

So when we see the daylight,
Which another night has won,
We will try to set all matters right
By worshipping the sun.

As we watch the passing faces
While the morning chokes and dies,
A thousand different places
May make us realise.

So you go home to mother
And I'll go home to bed,
But till you meet another
Remember all I said.

Meditations, on Chronos

The firework of delight began at four
And fizzled out at one,
The eternal law was kept
To gratify the sun.

When we woke at nine it seemed an age
Since Molly spilt her drink
On James's trousers,
And Tom had sat to think
About the problems
Of carousers.

Days

Across the plain
The days break rank,
Steal one by one
In glorious retreat.

Under the heavy treading
Of their feet
Hours and years run
Faster than the sun.

Busker

They laid him down into the lap of summer
The man from among the streets.

Into the earth under the wheat-waves
They laid him down,
Over the dead fields taken
Away from the town.

White stones sing no great tales,
Provide no clues in the aftermath,

No ballads born when body fails
Enough to pave his pauper-path
Chanted out under iron nails.

Seventy-odd

The pale yellow oranges of her breasts
               Bend under the high hill of her back.

The smarting cloud of her brown hair rests
               Beneath a battered judge-like hat of black.

A bloom in her blue eyes is not out
      Well-worn paths upon her cheeks only cringe and sag,

With some kind of leather smile about
               Latest bargains buried in her carrier bag.

Brown broken apples in her cheeks
               Can like summer sometimes blush with rage.

But usually she talks cheerfully, picks
               No quarrels with the bathos of her age.

Vision

Wind chases rain along the gutters,
Moans to the black flag of the sky,
Mutters through warmth down chimneys,
Breathing an outside murmur to eyes
Armchair-bound with surprise
That the warm smoke should blow about the room.

Matins

Charmed I'm sure
By your reply,

No, do not say more,
The essence of conversation
Reclines in a kind of lie.

When the morning shakes itself,
Wrings out its drenching pelt,
Perhaps changes its coat
In respect of emotion felt,
Falls giddily upon the throat
And asks, 'What is it all about?'

What can you reply
Except in a kind of lie?

This year lost its grace
When I saw its face
One morning grinning in a mirror.
Unshaven, unkempt as an errand boy.

Patterns

The white wet pearls
Fall one by one from the leaves
Into the pattern of the pool.

There to float for a moment
As on a cracked mirror

Where the silver is split
With concentric lines

As fine as a strain of silk
Whipped round with frost.

Kingfisher

My bizarre friend
Shining through the dark trees
That conceal your brightness,
Blend your hue
With the sun's falling,
Lend to the gold and blue
Your splendour.

Your crown matches the rainbow
With the river's silver ripple,
In your tumble down
Towards invisible fish.

Lord of the Flies

A bare wall beats down the sticky fly
Who pokes out tentative antennae.

Vertiginous height that can withstand
His bite and weight as
Down he falls to crush the floor.

He withers with the heat in the dusty
Rays of the sun,
Screaming in the silence with
Rustling of tiny tissues
Gnashing one against the other
With intolerable pressure.

Till all his breath is lost and
He lies crushed beneath the weight
Of the stuffy atmosphere,

Dust even as he lived he was,
Now nothing and not a single tear
To wipe away the stain
From the library floor.

Spider in a Jar

Now he forgoes the bite that once brought fear,
Cruel jar that makes him impotent with fright.

Brave brute
That almost without thought
Can understand the things he ought,
Struggling on in vain
With his spidery sort of pain.

He isn't quite fooled yet.
Yes, there he still runs round
His empty circus angry and amazed,
Despite the solemnity of his glass cage.

Perhaps he runs like a child
Spoiled in some silly game.

Perhaps he runs and runs like wild
To make us feel his shame, his fear,
As if it were our own, and we
Not him, were dying there.

From a City Window

(Homage to T S Eliot)

Funereal black-as-beetle chimneys
Those discoloured milk bottles
Light their dirty pipes.

The city smokes and wipes its nose
Upon a passing cloud.

Ants in blue whistle along the telescoped parallels,
Red and black toys bustle helter-skelter
Over the hustle
Of the noise.

Cacophony, like some strange bird,
Rips up the winter air into strips of rag,

Behind the blinds all the beauty of the world
Combs her perm and a little man
Waits, watches,

Waiting for his turn to prove
Himself a lady's man.

Beach-comb

Phalanxes of riches unattainable,
Ranks of the intangible,
Onto the sea's forehead crowd
In full battle order.

Emblems of earlier struggles,
Straggle of pearls and rubies,
Remnants of women forgotten
And girls chastised.

Past sentiment in ponds a shell of snail, whirl
Of broken ammonite and amethyst.

Crannies that waves
Had curled.

Lines of white stone, the broken lilies
Of the brine-land.

Flesh-marks, footprints in weed,
Bruised food for fish, coral seed,
Exotic symbolism of wrecked masts,
Accidents of mortality and need.

Flaming anemones, starfish,
Break-waters channelling jelly fish,
Brute rocks, wind wail, tide-bars,
Shawl of the cliffs, shards, seagulls' nests,
Trinkets filched from the sea's breasts.

In Whim or Design (1968)

Dale

In such fresh weather
When headstones lean
Uneasily in the yard,
Together we saw a rainbow
Straddling valleys like a sword.

Six summits smoked in mist,
Blue-smeared sheep paused curiously
To watch, their rumps stiff
Against the wind's fist.

We fed our eyes
Till it was spent form,
Confused by lines of light
Shaping the far skies movement.
Abruptly where grey houses
Were cupped in their dale's height
The sweet arc slipped from sight.

Behind us over bent rocks
Clouds flew low
Over the heath
Fast travelling like swans.
Stooped in a shooting box to watch
We felt flights of grouse
Gunned in the wind's teeth.

Ode to Daedalus

'Architectural in whim or design
To cage a monster or help a lover
His ethics were plausible, his fine
Intelligence an adjunct to industry,
His designs inspired to recover
A sense of decorum in times of degeneracy.'

Such an epitaph his new royal master
Might formally have summoned
On an occasion of national disaster.
Once the creator's son plummeted
In crazy vertigo into the sea's plaster –
Of-Paris lap, his sortie almost completed.

Heart-stricken an old man landed
Easefully on some deserted strip,
His voice heroically reprimanded
By Icarian arrogance, the lip
In mid-air pouting, then, stranded
Against the sun, a sudden wingless slip.
Having loved geometry and living things
His mind evolved toward movement.
Out of the labyrinth to spite kings.
What epitaph were adequate to circumvent
Such poetry? His elegant wings
Seem paradigms of all man might invent.

Crudely villainous in role and intent
Minos, not for the first futile time,
Turned his bureaucratic bent
To subtle experiment in crime,
To him, self-anointed in astonishment,
His plans seemed practically sublime.
Some vast pecuniary reward he said
Might go to the man who solved a riddle –
How to fill a twisted conch with thread
Right through its labyrinthine middle,
(Hardly a matter for those credited
With inventing flight, some taradiddle
A quite inferior mind might dream).

Daedalus in political asylum, bored
To tears, pleased to care for what might seem
A bogus scientific trick, poured
His grief to energy to redeem
Himself in blueprints at the drawing board.
He ran an ant right through the hole,
Unsensational like wax and feather.
King Minos read the signs, control
Of events assured, in pleasant weather
With bodyguards and protocol,
Minos and the Mafia talked together.
Perhaps that epitaph is Minos' alone,
The Sicilians were no fools, 'Daedalus stays',
Was their position; nothing more is known
But Minos died indecorously in a haze
Of myth in an alien drawing room,
Icarus avenged through another maze.

The ant still draws its thread;
Hall-marked those designations of his toil
Spite antiquity in lines old Ovid spread.

All Minos' many monsters could not spoil
The artificer's handiwork but instead
Augmented the Daedalian aureole.

Note to 'Ode to Daedalus'

Daedalus was an architect who designed a labyrinth for the Minotaur on the island of Crete; he showed Ariadne how Theseus could escape from the maze after Theseus had slaughtered the monster.

King Minos, as a punishment for Daedalus' impertinence, imprisoned the architect and his son Icarus in the labyrinth; escape by water and land were not possible but the sky was available. Daedalus made wings for his son and himself, and before take-off warned Icarus to maintain a reasonable altitude. The boy's excitement during the flight got the better of him and Icarus soared up towards the sun, thus melting the glue that held his wings, and plunging to his death in the sea.

Minos sought revenge for this escape. He proclaimed that a great reward would be given to the inventor capable of passing a thread through an intricately spiralled shell. Daedalus told the Sicilian king that he could manage this by boring a small hole in the closed end of the shell, fastening a thread to an ant, introducing the ant into the hole and then blocking up the hole; the ant emerged at the other end with the thread following him through the minute corridors. Minos realised that only Daedalus could have imagined such a plan and was killed after attempting to remove Daedalus from Sicilian asylum.

Requiem

Along the winding sheet of fields,
Where magpies march in martial search,
One morning in May when mist lay thick
I sought my love along the lane.

In mossed stone and rusty bark,
Splintered like old flesh,
At the crossroads' juncture
Near a town
I saw a sign of her sad pain.

A church invested with her dust,
A porch through which her sweet remains
Pauper-like in wood were thrust.

Death's dozen henchmen on the grass
Blackly watched
Quite unadorned her beauty pass.

In unfleshed stone her sound is said,
Words overgrown among sounds of birds
Searching for the long worm's head.

Eclogue

Into rurality to seek
Out of the town's drifting savour
Away from signs of streets or passers-by.
Swooping into deserted cottages
Lined with damp like blood
Into rooms as cold,
Old like corpses,
Whose chill fires could not dispel.
Not solitude to seek
And not to find.
Winter marked by cattle condemned,
Sick-lame with disease,
Barrows of two hundred head
Buried by disinfected men.
A stranded kitten perched
Like an apple in a palm
Screeched for its kin.
Sick sheep, hedgehogs rotted,
Weasels pinned out in the autumn,
Snow beating from unlighted hills
Across sepulchral trees.
Such is not solitude or heart's ease.
Returns to places or familiar marks,
Successful friends in townish apartments,
Scatterings of shops and lights,
Confused searchings out of bearing,
Sang strange mentionings to mind
Returned us to some found land
Of new-discovered substance.

Under that sky's sweep
In country struggle
Comfortably isolated,
We note the bullfinch hesitate,
Bark blister in frost,
A garden's pinched cheek wimpled in grin,
A score of old nests in so many yards,
Daily disturbance of mortality,
Field, fluff, feather, flesh, or fur.

Hard to settle for less than these happenings,
A thrush's cataclysm with the snail corpse,
Familiar trees in their moods.

Swaledale, Yorkshire

Ambiguous marks, shapes, lines
Of shadows, forms without breath
Into sunlight out of sunlight stretching
From green to grey to graciousness;
Not to live in such land
When having lived
Is spare parting, a harking
Back to shepherds suckling orphan lambs
To goats, to sheer sweep of
Owned deserted acres
Some cited street cannot forgive.
Fallow those hills, purple with old
Blood; sheep and birds
After the fighting possess
Utterly their dumpy dunes
Entrenched after the lead gods left
Or fled
Or metamorphosed subtly out of sight,
Though their dim faces still
Obtain among some shallow valleys;
From a long mile's throw a limp spot
On the land hauls his weight against
An incline's spite,
His whistles chatter
Round his fleet dog's spoor
Against that hill-cut sky.
Desolate birds before the breeze
Above brute rocks
Drift in brisk frieze.

Beach

Perplexed
Caught
Between a mountain's negation of tenderness
Their sea's obscure beauty

Winter gulls cavort uneasily
In a sky's twirled lines

Form torn from bewilderment
They whoop like children
Over beaches deserted

To slip
Along the waves' arched backs
Looking into eye of sea unflinchingly
To pick at spines of fish that light refracts

Out of a cold wind's bellying
In troughs for split seconds
To shelter
And stall

Their spare singing of consent
Spins out
The fall.

Pastoral

Birds fly
Informally above the fields
Swallows in evening dress stoop low
Over many flight paths

Grass hides the dirt
And elsewhere
Wheat beckons as if enervated
And the common snail sings to the thrush ill at ease
In its brown shift

Bold wealds in country colours call
A whisper of dew can shake the earth
(But our ears are stopped)

Birds call
Unrestfully above the fields
Grass in heat shows dust

Mown wheat falls in the fields
White waves flatten under our feet

Snails have crawled
Away from their shields
Their husks as shells on a shore
Sit informally in our path.

Dog

A crinkly dog without a lead,
Along long lanes of rural state,
Treads elegantly those lines of leaves
Through which he loves to ambulate.

His feet are crotchets in the green,
His pride the pride of love possessed,
His bark to bitches all around
Music of strange tenderness.

Within his colour-blinded world
A colour percolates the nose,
Among those lanes where lovers wait
His bitches emulate the rose.

The good task done, his deed complete,
He moves to fields of fresher fame.
Shrill hedgerows and sweet musk rose
Share the flavours of his game.

In heights of trotting dignity
He moves through lines of cheering trees,
Quaint sounds of birds, soft hints of dew,
Augment his sensuous avenue.

Austrian Incident

Hemmed in by peaks
Upon a broken pitch,
The football coach,
His eyes half on the match,
Rolled up his sleeve
To show a number Auschwitz
Printed in his flesh.

A scruffy patch
Of skin, like leather
Punctured round,

Or like a scar of grass
On barren ground.

Childhood

We wove a web in childhood,
A web of sunny air,
We dug a spring in infancy
Of water pure and fair.
CHARLOTTE BRONTË (1816–55)

War Baby

Tiny through tall grass
I listened to the whimpering wind,
Climbed enormous trees,
Rode in heart to cloud summit
Like a bird,
And to Gogmagog Hill,
Lime Kiln Spinney,
And the Roman road
Traced feet in summer dust.

I saw monsters in skies
Long shadows of chariots,
Grasses hissed with snakes
Fear sang through creaking branches.

Once, trapped in storm behind bushes,
The scraggy stuffed bear
With his one glass eye
Comforted me.

In the garden of smallness
The head imagines no bullets
Or the accumulated dead,
Planes zing into the blue like dragonflies
Never to sting with gently camouflaged wings.
While millions died
My only evil was that big brown rat,
Squat under the garden shed
With long tail and wicked whiskers.

Girl

You grew up beautiful,
Straight, patient and watching,
Tasting of apricots, blackberries and blossom,
Magically touching in eye, voice and being,
Resonating in me like a sea-bell.

I open the cage of my heart,
Where you are for ever trapped,
To urge you, sweet bird, sweet skylark,
Please go.

Children's Playground

Dark bobbins in dusk
Boys swing in the distance,

Their invisible chains clank
Across an arc of decaying song.

Dying day drives them,
A sudden snatching fall,
The twist through wet air
With bent legs against the half-light
Bird-like but tethered,
To swoop down to darkening grass and
Up, up from earth's pulling,
Worlds sink at the body's urge gut-shrinking
Then the fall back.

Birds shriek shielded
By dogs calling
And the last child-sounds echo.

But seen from a distance,
Without support, defiant,
They fall rise fall, eerie in twilight,
Shapes moving camouflaged,
Chameleon, towards night's colours
Pitching against the dark.

I Mother

(1979)

Mother, I do not, cannot,
Recall (all memory tossed into time's pit),
You, your body, or your face.
Before four years old (strange time)
You cast me to the stranger's net,
And so without familiar flesh
I move on earth,
Never to meet, or knowing to have met.

That seal you set on us (and I regret).
Now forty years
Split the continents of our humanity,
We do not share the voyage towards death,
Exile and the lengthening seas
Dispose our lives.
Mother, you live in silence,
As if long dead,
Only remains name and life,
Solitary good gifts to have
While the blood runs.

Mother, though I cannot recall you,
Or return shape or sound
To the womb's race,
Beneath the folds of time
I dream of union never severed
By word or bad weather,
So (in some sense or other) the cord holds
And we remain together.

II   The Meeting

"Your guest is in reception"
They rang up to say,
Sunlight in the voice.

Along the world's longest corridors I move,
Down stairs so deep they freeze the blood,
From darkness to the sun,
Through doors as heavy as planets.

She was seated patiently.
"Hello, how lovely to see you," (me, kissing
Her unknown cheek),
"Let's go upstairs.
Can you manage stairs?
So many of them here."
"Of course, I live with stairs."

Reaching through the maze to Room Sixteen
I forget what was said or seen.

Only endless corridors stretching,
The two of us between.

Till in the room, grey haired, small,
She, stranger and mother, told all.

III Looking and Touching

"You never take your eyes from me
You touch me as if I'll vanish into air."

Forgive me if I look at you
Forgive me if I stare

You are the picture I forgot
Image of all I want to know,

I read you like a new book
Therefore I must look.

Not a single thing must go
There is so much to know.

Touching face or cheek or hair
Keeps you from not being there.

IV The Return

(1990)

"You must harbour some hatred, some resentments,"
She said flatly, not with rancour,
But factually as facts come.

"Most certainly not, not a single one."

But unaccustomed images run
With discoveries of blood,

Strange tricks of light in transition
From darkness to the sun.

A Boy and a Dog

I

I always live as if I'm going to leave quite soon
(Friends, town or some strange country),
It may come from experiences out of mind
Some time when golden-curled and cute
A look was not enough to capture love,
Or help me stay by love's great root,
Where we should be – a mother's heart,
The place of motherhood.

Having sown his seed
Irish dad joins the army and soon dies
(Not bullets in back or breast,
Uniformed tuberculosis gave him rest)
And in a war grave now he lies.

II

To Coventry – until the German visit.
That night she leaves the shelter
Where all will die, blasted, wasted,
Driven she runs dark noisy streets,
(You'd think such entwinings might seal our bond
But worse would come,
A baby son is not always welcome home).

We go to Cambridge town
Looking to her future and things,
But living with a sister
Cramps wings.

III

At work she finds a hanging body,
Thinks of ma and pa dead
When she was ten,
A girl of no worth,
Time to think and grieve,
Her parents' double death
Her son's unwelcome birth.

IV

A childless couple hover,
Mum passes the parcel over,
Enamoured with a lover,
Jack the lad, demobbed, the rover,
Yearns and clamours for my quick release
(Barnado's or some other bourne
From which no little traveller returns)
And so at three the cord is cut,
Caesarean odyssey.

V

Space, curtains, in the mind,
Divide what came from what stayed behind,
A morning flit, unexplained,
Separating everything and me
Where sense of pleasure was at an end
For moving house from a to b
The silly men forgot my gun,
My joy, my precious friend,
Loved with reverence, the best of fun,
Yes, they forgot to take my darling gun.
To my new overlords I appeal,

Oh could we but return to look,
To that empty house not far away,
Where something in the dust and dirt
Could heal the substance of my hurt
By bringing back the thing I love to clutch,
And so with tears
I ask too little and too much,
Just, this moment, please to go,
But every tantrum strengthened no,
And though the supplication's real
Time's dilemma does not heal.

What's lost is lost with no returns,
The forest of the child destroyed
For ever burns.

VI

Yet from that burning, a hungry phoenix comes,
Young hearts are full of good,
Despite the odds
There was a house,
A garden and a dog.
Finger to the wind, among much shifting sand,
I cling to the dog as early sailors did to land.
The art of navigation's hard
But having failed the game
Count gain not loss.
For in the flickering fadings of our days
Pieces on the board will change
But the board stays.

VII

I pose with the dog,
Looking out for ever from that sepia tinge,
Sweet Nella growling by my side.

Once in the sitting room,
Too weak to walk, she passed
A sticky turd to the mat.

I called for them to come,
They came too late,
She took it in her mouth
Gulped it back,

Poor dear animal.

Mythologies

I made my song a coat
Covered with embroideries
Out of old mythologies
From heel to throat...
> WILLIAM BUTLER YEATS (1865–1939)

Ancien Régime

The cauldron sings Telemachus
Is dead, where he should stand before the hearth
A daughter cries.

And black with weeping for the missing
Dead are those town-tipped eyes.

While wood breathes deep from the chimney
As the cauldron prays and bubbles,
Spitting fits of water onto resentful ashes.

Boiling tears clash on the hearth,
All is envisaged as a man's face for
Tired owl-like eyes.

While rows of pearls and beads are pulled
Along a rosary warm from the fire,
Hot stones to touch with wet fingers.

While a man's face crumbles in the pyre
Of sticks and a woman
Wipes her eyes and licks
Cold salty lips.

Requiem for Orpheus

At the end a peculiar horror,
Tearing out his lyrical tongue
Maenad ruffians silenced his sorrow.

Later in wild terror
They tossed to Hebrus
A severed head
(Once he had sung songs to turn
Insanity to dream).

Though water like time
Consumes rock or flesh,
No flood could lash
To lack of shape his curly head.
So on a magic beach
Quaint gods might fish,
Whole from their sea's mouth,
A mask of the dead.

Buried at last in earth
He receives his wish
(As nightingales lament his name).

In Eurydicean bliss
He concludes desire,
Not to recover her from death
But to be the same.

Odysseus

Between two seas
His tiny ship is caught.
One (looking back
From the wave-struck stern),
Discerns the debris
Of past voyages,

While from the crow's nest,
With straining eyes,
The cabin boy, in shrill ecstasy,
Proclaims the coming tide of pain
At the horizon's edge.

Skies

Like illuminated fish
Clouds float on into fresh skies.
Pegasus steered in such content,
Through space poor Icarus careered.

The openness of skies naturally
Tethers winged horses to clouds,
Or spins heroes towards the sea,
Primevally stormy.
Easy then to hear gods utter threats,
Or Thor's anvil striking sparks,
Or Christ's lament to a blackened sky.

Another hour
Perhaps the sun's bullet
Splinters a blue wholeness.
In lighter immensity.
Wave-forms or shark-spined shreds
Image from abstract to shape.
In that vast sea without sound
A bearded Neptune's fluffy trident shows,
Speared in foam.

At night all shades
Shift through red dusk to dark,
Moonlight clutters the eyes.

We pick over human paths
Blind in the sky's moor.

Apollo

Was it autumn then when in pursuit
Of Daphne's lovely shape
Apollo chased through groves of fruit,
Flowers, the ripening grape?

Did pears hang high and berries
Beckon, tempting among the trees?
Of course no man would pick at cherries
When his divine objective flees.

What mattered was the race,
Gods are not beaten in a game of dice,
Apollo in that moment set the pace,
Reached out rapaciously to seize the prize.

But at his grasp the evening woods went dark
And Daphne's fruit-like flesh, breasts, legs and thighs,
Face, eyes, everything, all changed to tree and bark.

Western

Possession of cattle,
The steer-rich ground,
Formed identity.

Scaped by a hot land
They grew solitary,
Resisted psychos
Or followed strong heroes.

In simple honesty
They sought their inner selves,
Or fought across acres
Against intruders.

Accustomed to slaughter
Under a primeval sky,
They saw the bison diminish,
The red men murdered.

Myth is always a matter of guilt,
A shaping of images.
Moments of sharp light
Like spines of cactus
Caught by the moon
At the desert's edge.

Birthday

Yeats's 'gold mosaic' still delights,
Or Grecian urn, that artefact
Which over centuries of nights
Resonates, fragile but uncracked.

Not like our short days, disappeared,
(Sleepers beneath a moving train),
For relief see monuments sheered
From rock, immune against the rain.

Or mosaics in a palace,
Entirety patched from fragments,
(Our sums of decades don't tell us
Complete tales tallied from segments).

So we have lived, so will we die,
In bits, pieces, disconnected,
Till in sweet memory we lie
Forlorn, atomised, dissected.

Mosaic walls, urns, persevere,
(Enchanted, each living eye looks).
We linger out the passing year,
Sentences in unfinished books.

This birthday is a piece of glass
In the mosaic of my days,
I see no form within the mass,
I read each word but not the phrase.

Judgement

Three beings abandon that elegant dawn
Between a swallow's spiral and the sea,
Some old woman cursing against a coming storm,
A saint indulged in prayer along the shore,
A virgin beyond imaginings exquisite in her form,
In trinity they tread towards a dreadful door.

Ugly as rocks or browed waves, doomed to age,
That breastless virago stumbles out of sight,
Unwillingly first under the lintel for her wage
She shifts stiff limbs in painful pace,
Too numbed for shame or sense, yet rage,
Forgetfulness and fear still smear her face.

The saint's gait purports small sin,
All's moved into the chapel of his heart,
Yet he too follows where she entered in.
Though she was blindly saddened by grief
He feels some kinship, for beneath his skin
Blood beats wild like the sea despite belief.

Drawn towards reverie the virgin moves
Out of a cold sea-wind into a soft space.
She sings familiar songs of one she loves,
Straight and holy as a tree he is, warmer than the sun.
Before the door she pauses to imagine his embrace,
Then white-breasted like a swan, enters silent as a nun.

Duet

A man who has murdered,
Or some saint,
In each respective cell.
When mist tainted distant hills,
Or frost touched the bars with silver,
To each his own remonstrances.

(Along blue tremors of watery sky
Long birds mirror in the glassiness.
They stoop low over waves
Those lone inquisitors,
A second mars or saves
Each trivial moment of a passing fish
From beak or pike
Or breakfast dish.)

This man remembers lethal force,
A stab of conscience the other,
On tentative knees, scarred with remorse.

Reflections

Dear Narcissus gazing at the pool
Saw such beauty there as never seen before.
They'd known him as a lovely boy at school,
The prettiest creature shaped for lover's lore.
Now if he'd been an ugly little sprog,
Misshapen nose, bad teeth and horrid skin,
The water's mirror would refract him like a frog
And horrified he might have fallen in.
Rather he glimpsed the finest beauty of the earth,
And human-like fell straight in love with that instead,
His love of loveliness, right from its birth,
Romantically deflected all reflections in his head.
Till pondering on the glories of that sight
Where could he go but down and down?
Too much in love to drink or take a bite,
In such reflection he began to drown.
The message of the pool was all too much,
Love was a mirror of that boy's complexion,
But could such love once felt so touch
One's life, that nothing else could matter but reflection?
Whatever the answer to that awkward question,
Narcissus pining died, and changed into a flower.
He would have been appalled at the suggestion
That love like his was not worthwhile but sour.

For love like his seems worth it for the fond,
And love is blind and love is inauspicious –
Oh, Reflets dans l'eau float gently on your pond,
For in your glassy eye I look just like Narcissus!

—

Memorial

Hoof-prints in the red dust
Mark the psychopath's grave.

A crude cross betrays the savour of death,
Thorns of cactus snap light,
Their stark sculptures, leaves like spears,
Thrust to the sun in heroic pose.

The Sea

The dragon-green, the luminous, the dark,
the serpent-haunted sea…
THE GATES OF DAMASCUS, WEST GATE
JAMES ELROY FLECKER (1884–1915)

December Ship

The ship crawls like a lizard
Over the sea,
The sun pauses,
Catches it in a beam.

Is this the Archangel Gabriel?
Or just a ship which comes
Home every year,
To light a candle
In a faithful woman's heart?

Lyrical Ballad

Take ship, my love,
On wider seas than these,
Take ship.

Follow tall seas
Towards the palm
Brooding green against blue
With deceitful claim.

Or watch the pied snake
Curl under the bough,
Watch the scorpion wake.

Take ship, my love, now.

Thoughts after a Swim

Half dry on a long beach,
Lemons of waves attack naked feet,
Toes wrinkle in retreat.

Over the watery alleys of waves
Desultory birds shave the spray,
They have no past to name,
No unfortunate moments of recall,
Theirs but to watch the waters rise and fall.

Unfriendly hills gesture at the sea,
Mist hugs their green gravelly breasts,
The incoming tide drums in the creek,
Against the sea's sound a watch ticks.

Night Glimmers

A fabulous moon
(An eyeball over a silver sea)
Tells what it has seen
Of lovers
And departed sailors.

In Memoriam...

And now we know,
As surely as the waters
Of this tiny stream flow
To rivers and the broad estuary.

We too shall go.
Already we
Almost hear the sea.

Ship

Carried forward, we think
From yesterday, or days before,

How for weeks the sea
Has surrounded, overwhelmed.

We are its plaything now.
Even as the deep calmly sleeps
We watch its face,
Wait for its mouth to open.

Horizons spotted with rain,
Sun-splashed.

Sailor's Love Song

I love you deeper
Than seas are deep,

I love you higher
Than waves are high,

I love you longer
Than journeys are long,

I love you further
Than horizon and sky.

I love you warmer
Than south winds are warm,

I love you fresher
Than hot apple pies,

I love you more happily
Than a sailor's laugh,

I love you more sadly
Than the tears in my eyes.

Suicide Note

Having fallen from a liner,
Into the China Sea,
I float free.

My body will not let me down,
I shall swim till I sink
And then drown.

Facing the waves
With joy and fear,
Sailing cork-like towards infinity,
I taste salt water rinsing me,
A sea breeze ruffles my hair.

Hardly a cloud in the sky I see,
Though somewhere the sun
Catches a plane passing by,
They cannot see me,
Like a fish it is my wish
To stay here till I die.

All I want from death is loneliness,
And if my soul flies up like a bird
Not a word nor scream will be heard.

In this sea the end is endlessness.

Song of the Drowning Man

Tossed and lost among waves I ride,
In the boisterous sea,
Hungry waves grow higher and higher,
Embracing me.

I throw up my arms and wait to sink
Like a bride to a silken bed.

The final cries are uttered,
The last prayers are said.

Song of the Mariner

Year after year
We endure
The sea's embrace,
Its voice, its fear,
Its taste.

The Drowned Girl

The white-women of the sea held her
In their ugly arms.

The white-women washed her, stroked her,
Cloaked her, choked her,
Tossed her,
Washed her no more.

The salt-men rubbed their bitter brine
Into her eyes.

The sandmen sent soft sands
Into her hair.

The seamen kept their distance
From the wake,
Watching her cold corpse there.

Seascape

Today the sea is a sheet of blue glass,
Sweet under the sky's embrace,
A streak of cloud runs in the air,
Gulls wheel and pass.

Earlier a weak sun
Shed silver flecks like ice
Against the water's face.

Sunset

The sun dropped
Into a marmalade sea.

We watched
For the fall.
The sky reddened
Like a shy girl.

A runner round the deck stops short,
Tells us about running,
Eyes bright in sunset,
Remembering marathons,
'Blood pressure perfect,
At sixty fit for anything.'

By the tale's end
The sun has shrivelled
To tiny oyster flesh,
And the sky is mildly pink.

Voyage

See how the billows sweep
From the bow,
Tresses of a passionate woman or
Floating in patterns, bubbling
Vortexed, blue crystals,
Away to the distance,
Joining the streaming mane
Towards the stern
As far as the eye strains
To limits of the vastness.

So with love's memory
From the instant to distance,
Lost in seas of feeling,
All details carried to the darkness,
Moved more than mind can hold
To things lost.

Forgotten words of another language
Streaming back to youth's infinity,
Away from this afternoon's sharp edge.

Walk

Along this beach
Rain beats my face,
The wind is a clenched fist.

Dark waves
Sob like children.

As far as the eye can see
Ships slip like memories
Into mist.

Sea Mood

This evening's sighing of the sea,
(Grey waves shifting ill at ease,
A light mist filtering till eyes cannot see),
Fills the soul with images
Of being young in that breeze,
Setting sail under a cheerful sky.

This evening's chant
In all its lovely loneliness,
Tolls out, tells
What is lost, gently,
Like telling a child
Of unfathomable loss.

Meeting

The sailor with a wistful smile,
"How strange, it's three years
Since I saw your face,
Three years since our last embrace."

The woman standing at the door,
"Why do you say three years
When you mean four?
Four years I waited,
Watching the winding
Road to the sea.

Come in, but remember the child
You'll find here,
Belongs now only to me."

Sea Sleep

It's strange how when you sleep
And then wake up
The world has changed,
The squall has gone, dreams have gone,
And is that daylight coming on?

But no, I'm still at sea and
Soon it's time to muster up on deck,
To blink at the blood-shot sky.
(What watch it is I wouldn't know
Or to what God-forsaken port we go.)

Lulled on the drowsy deep,
For now I'll fall back into sleep.

Wave Watcher

What do you see, wave watcher?
The sun's footsteps traced in silver,
Ships sailing far apart.

What can you hear, wave watcher?
The ocean tolling like a bell,
Sighing like a broken heart.

Letter

How sad
My ship
Did not
Reach harbour.

Beaten back
I look
Towards your land,
Where breezes
Ruffle your hair,
And sun
Lights your eyes.

Where together we would have hunted
The lost dove
Of love,
In dark forests
Far from the sea.

Night Sea

Ships like candles twitch,
A buoy winks its eye,
Waves off the leash,
Bite, bit by bit, at the cliff's flesh.

Splash salts the lips,
At the edge no light.

Everywhere
The weather is falling apart.

Sea Night

Night holds us in its centre,
Oh imagine floating alone
Among such moonless black!

Just thinking is to be there,
Even as we sing or touch another's hand
Against the dark.

Journey

In conflux of tide
Where river flow
And sea's pull collide
We paddle our coracles of flesh.

Thin insubstantial boats, not
Sufficient to last out all
Storm, weakening against
Successive waves.

But for all that, in their element,
As tiny fish swim deep, so far
Horizons and harbours retreat,
Buoy up the soft craft and
Before we sink, wildly we float,
Corky survivors in the sea's mouth.

Flamborough Head

Little waves lead
The inward tide,
Seeping shyly
Across rocks and weed.

As if the softly singing beach
Hums some old sailor's song,

Who sleeps for ever
In that whispering sea.

Voyage

I prepare my boat
To float to the ocean,

To reflect there
On what tides bring.

Over the sea
Gulls will sing
Of lost days.

Winds have shifted,
We are far from land.

Ebbing away,
Unknown, unspoken for,

In sea-darkness.

Viking Funeral

Then is his body burned,
Over an evening sea the husk glows
After torches thrust into an oak hull,
Float, waste, among sea wastes,
Here the soul drifts ocean-seeking,
Sunset bloods the blaze,
Small hot star against the waves,
Hungry for eternity, bright brief planet
Fired in gathering night.....
Cinders, ashes, spears, earth-remnants,
A sleeping sword deep-sheathed, sea-bound,
Tide-blown body, wind-lifted, where flames
Whisper to an outgoing flood, a shower
Of bitter sparks tossed against scorched sail,
Ash-littered water where cold dark fills the
Sea's edges, that fire-ship takes wing to her
Horizon's spread, lost years away at last sent seaward.
Then at dawn is that lost ship
Not yet sunk, though burned bare to bone,
Rib and spar, strangely sailing, charred
Raft, a bitter barrow, spent wood, the
Ravaged ash of carving, the profaned prow...
But all flesh consumed, all glory, and
Watchers weary with waking, wave-smitten
Wreck of memory, all nerves taut in half-light,
See, heat-twisted lifted images of past life,
Out of time forced, out of turn,
Now look strong into the sea's face
Till eyes ache sore and burn.

A Sailor Remembers

I miss you more than words can say,
More than songs can sing,
I miss you more than sunset,
More than coming spring.
I miss you more than autumn,
More than dreamy sleep,
I miss you more than birdsong,
Or the company I keep
I miss you more than morning,
More than stars and moon,
I miss you more than ever,
Every afternoon.
I miss you more than sunshine,
More than summer heat,
I miss you more than rain or snow,
Or the food we eat.
I miss you every moment,
From dawn to dusk and more,
I miss you in the silence,
Or in the ocean's roar.
I miss everything about you,
As I watch the waves around,
I shall miss you now for ever,
Who was lost and never found.
I miss you more than words can say,
More than songs can sing,
More than the gull's wail,
Or the deep sea's sighing.

Places and Journeys

Will the day's journey take the whole long day?
From morn to night, my friend.

UP-HILL
CHRISTINA ROSSETTI (1830–1894)

Thoughts in Malta

I

A leaden sun sinks
Its heat in blue placidity.
Those waters absorb
A lighted sky
Like a mirror of sponge.
Habitations too repel
The casual skin.
On flat roofs at mid-day
The sun is an aimed needle.

II

A brown girl twists like a fish
Through blue modulations.
Seen from a shaded balcony,
Her flesh swims cool
In the silvery blue water.

III

My white body is a scar on these sands,
Prone in the beach's lap
I search motionless towards gaunt shrub
And the sculptured horror of cactus
For the beneficence of shade.

IV

In thin scraps of twisted wire,
Across heated paths,
Skinny lizards intermittently shift,
Still as slim stones or quick as fearful fish.

Song of the Spanish Saint

(Palma, Mallorca)

Below her golden hem of dress
Skeleton feet, skinless hands,
A bonneted skull caressed
By silky drapes and silver bands.

Eye-catching, the anatomised girl,
Lavishly tombed, trapped by glass,
Mocks the watcher's covered curl,
Grins coyly as men move to Mass.

"Here will I lie upon my back,
Bride-clothed in Spanish lace,
Nothing I am, nothing I lack
Except the soft flesh of my face."

Short Story

Like migrant geese,
Having explored unknown places,
A traveller and his companion
Found an enchanted lake,
Brimmed with trees,
Sheltered by hills,
Dreamily calm.

Day after day
They boated its immense mirror,
Fished or watched tranquil faces
Imaged in its clarity.

They built a cabin
By an elegant shoreline.
Night after night
They slept in peace,
Under the mountain's eye.

One morning,
When rain shifted like birds' feet
On the roof,
The lake eased its length,
In languid waves splashing the beach,
Fish floated bellies upwards,
Like silver ribbons.
Dead geese drifted, ragged feathered dolls,
A dying moose struggled for breath
After drinking,

Beyond the trees a rainbow
Ironically decorated the distance.

Burning their poisoned cabin,
Stealthily they departed
To the western reaches,
Where lakes proliferate.

Salvador, Brazil

Slicing through the bay's virginity
We edge, big eyed, between moored ships,
Towers like fingers gloved in the mist,
Castanet cameras click, binoculars jostle.

Ashore we meet our match,
Welcoming girls, men, ribbons,
A dance to the mad song of taxis.

For this we came? Yes,
But here is strangeness
More hazardous than the sea's kiss.

Driving through Valencia, Spain

Orange orchards
Stretching to the sea,

Blue-topped breakers
Singing on the shore.

Pearl River in the Rain

Heavy through Hangchow
The dirty river drifts,

Carrying rusty ships and junks
In its black mouth.

This snake never will stop eating
Till the land is devoured,
Or the dark rain lifts.

India

As if for all time all springs dried,
Till the red soil like deficient skin
Split slowly into sores and died.

In silence birds
Crouch in dust,
To watch rats eat turds.

In that heat's sweep,
Insects desolately creep,
Huge wasps sting each other into sleep.

A white cow cracked twigs between weak sacred teeth,
Its arse putrid like clay decayed,

Children thinner than the skinny limbs of trees
Basked pot-bellied in its holy shade.

Leningrad

Here where river, ice, history,
And our lives,
Meet – that black ship
Bulks large in the night.

Manacles of cold
Bite our legs,
In this grip
We stand by the white Neva.

And a long frozen blocked river
Begins in our bellies,
Like a sleeping serpent,
To unwind.

Leaving the Falklands

These waters are sad,
Beautiful as light changing.

Silver slivers of sun
Dazzle like fish in the evening ocean.

Clouds change,
Touching mountain tops with orange.

The town crouches like a child, red and blue,
Green hills reel back.

These waters are sad,
Beautiful as light changing.

Journey

Eyes closed tight,
Against the light of clouds,
I dreamed of voyaging
Through chalcedonic seas,
Where each sharp wave grew
Flower-like from beds of silver,
Each curve of sea
Soft-tinted in sun.

Our ship moved
Towards a setting dusk of blue and red,
Every shiver of the ship
Soothing like a body
Dipped in silk.

I woke, the plane leapt
Like a frightened horse
Jumping at the sun.

Andalusia

Sunned tired body,
Like a bull on whose
Soft flesh picadors feasted.

The sun's lance slows, loosens,
Orange heaviness, till skin
Flowers red passionate blossoms,
Like lightly drawn swords on the body,
Sun-sores, censorious wounds,
Skin-deep, savage.

Lakeside at Night

Water flickers
In the lake bowl,
Stars pick holes.

Dark breasts of land
Feed and lullaby,
Water flickers.

Mongolian Lamasery

A smell like stabled
Beasts, they sit in
Rows, yellow parchment faces,
Saffron robes give off
A sweet, sickly fragrance…

They sing, strike bells,
Chant deep or high,
The prayerful pages peel
One by one, and when the
Young monk lights each
Candle with a gentle
Touch, old men crouch,
Like obedient still children
Nuzzling the Lama's robe.

Our guide, a devout
Communist, looks at his watch,
Signals us out.

Ilmington Village

In the church a Gershwin
Song augments the summer festival,
The soprano holds until a breath
Runs off the note, she can be
Heard a dozen bushes off, here in
An old country, where the land sucks
Greenly at the sense, and walled gardens
Sink their secrets into warm earth.

Midges scout the summer air
Or tease the young calves, the manor
Gardens spring an Augustan glimpse,
Among orchards the still sheep sprawl,
Roses like fountains from the houses fall.

Here is ironic summertime before a fall,
Gushed blossom from the yellow stone,
The short-grassed ancient grave.

Here sense and time collude,
We move gently for here time is free,
And the clock a liar.

The Long Journey

(For Iryna, about to emigrate)

Bird-like over the sea
It is time to go,
And though the heart
Pulls back like a stone
To things known, secret wings beat
Forward always into dark and light,
Like a song heard against the wind.

No retreat, only the heart's desire
For movement and flight,
Strange dawns rising like fire.

Calcutta

Sometimes when eyes meet between strangers,
In the passing dance of a street,
Things happen.
One-sided it may be,
This passing current of a kind of touching,
Perhaps I noticed, perhaps one looked but never saw
Or wanted not to see,
Or in the case of a girl
I saw her extraordinary
Beauty, and she saw that I had seen.
I certainly saw him and his arms responded to me,
His young eyes were expressive as a river,
And like flowing water reached to me.
I saw him and my eyes sank deep into him,
My eyes were stones in the current of his stream,
Stone-like my eyes were flung into his life,
His boy's arms like a dying swimmer reached to me.
But I saw him with ten companions around him,
Who swam with him, breathed with him,
Drowned with him,
And to favour him was to disfavour them,
And I passed,
Leaving them all to lie there in life's hideous river.
He stares at me still in rivers of dream,
I remember eyes,
Arms most expressive.
As our eyes met in the dance of the street,
His beautiful eyes, his body
Without legs, begged.

Algiers

This square is a white
Polished mirror,
Reflecting up
To the sun-glassed eye.

Even when averting sight
Up to the silver mosque,
Legless beggars
Sting like scorpions
On the hot skin.

Goats in the Trees

(Moroccan Suite)

Tangier Morning
The waking sun leaves
gold prints on the bay,
a hundred dogs
bark at the dawn.

The Street of Shadows
Shadows flee like driven sheep
before the coming light,
they creep into the ends of streets
to sleep till it is night.

The Street of Secrets
Once in this street
a young man snatched his love
(a plucked rose)
from her father's side.
None saw them ever again,
neither the bridegroom nor the bride.

Goats in the Trees
Like ghosts the goats perch in the trees
(blossom against an overheated sky),
they bleat like bells and pose like birds
as if about to fly.

The Mosque
That sunlit tower
begs a thousand questions.
None will be answered
while we stand outside the gate.

Fruit Stall Vendor
Come buy my peppers, hot or sweet,
and I will sing you the song
they sang a thousand years ago,
when the world was young.

Pots in the Sunlight
Pots squat like pilgrims on the ground
Round mouths open in surprise,
They have no tongues and cannot speak
Which makes them infinitely wise.

Blue Fishing Boats in Essaouria
After this,
one dream
one wish
blue boats float on
tides of silver fish.

Garden

In such a garden
a poem could be written.
No need, this garden
is already a poem of love.

Pots and Pans in the Souk

Metal tinkles in the filtered light,
like drums and cymbals hung up high,
strange music fills the ear and eye,
and whispers to each passer-by.

The Palace in Tetuan

With six golden chariots
and twelve silver horses
the King has come home.
The King's in his palace,
all's well with the world.

Night

The mosque light glows and greets
a blood-moon sky.
Midnight. Silence
touches the garden and the streets.

Australia

The red berry of our autumn sun
Is now the orange bud of spring,

Starlings become cockatoos
Tuhy birds in eucalyptus sing.

Through the fields leap kangaroos,
Parakeets take wing,

And there a sly echidna scurrying.

American Suite

(Homage to Walt Whitman)

Broadway

New York, New York,
We shall in idle talk
Recall
How on the sidewalk
A madman
Leaped in amusement.
Did he have a knife?
New York, New York.

Unshaped for life
A massive man
Fat as barrels
Browsed among pictures
Of slim women.
New York, New York.

Walk, don't walk,
Walk, don't look too hard,
Talk, not too loud,
New York, New York,
Ugly faces in the crowd,
Stare. Always there.

Beacons in the sea,
Dangers in a flood,
Poison in good blood,
New York, New York,

We move in fear,
Our dark destined angel
May be near,
And who
Of all these faces
Is his messenger?

Washington – *At the Lincoln Memorial*

We are washed in heat
From the blue pan of the sky,
Up-thrust of marble.
We are sandwiched in warmth,
Grass glows green heat
And the sucking fountains mock.
At this shrine and demi-tomb
Pilgrimage we assume.
Here and across the Potomac
Many bullets have found flesh.
This whiteness of steep stone
Is bone-white,
Where the great martyr sits
And others sleep in Arlington.

What washed stone
Shaped in the mind's heat
Makes meaningful
This stone's silence?
Cold as crushed ice
In the mouth is truth,
History, heavy as heat,
Sits on our backs.

Statue of Liberty

Thrust your flame,
Green goddess,
A writing fist
Into the smoky sky,
Your stone eyes
Look to the sea.
Against your back
The unfathomable land,
While under the gateway
Small ships slip,
Gouged from the sea's mouth.

One day distant
Fist and flame
May fall into the bay,
Your brave arm wearied,
Worn away.

Then, oh magnificent ruin of dream,
Riven, time-broken, like humanity,
Never would you from the sea
Be dredged.

Instead stand
Wounded, fistless,
An imagined torch
Uplifted
At the ocean's edge.

Song of the Statue of Liberty

Why did I not wake till now?
Was it the giant's touch I lacked?

In Europe I was a sleeping princess,
I longed for America to change me into flesh.

Here in my hand the torch breaks into flame,
A million dawns burn bright with brilliant light,
As in the sky I scorch our sacred name.

New York Love Song

Your body vibrates
Like the city,
Your intersections,
Highways,
Skyways,
Sidewalks,
Run with summer heat.

No use waiting
On street corners
Admiring silky gestures,
The flashing lights.

Set off downtown
To secret hideaways,
Till we approach the deep,
And
Gently
Gently
Gently
Parachute
Into sleep.

Creatures Great and Small

All things bright and beautiful,
All creatures great and small,
All things wise and wonderful,
The Lord God made them all.
    Cecil Frances Alexander (1818–1895)

Hedgehog

Reggie Hedgehog
Eats the beetles
One by one,
One by one.

Walks across
The moonlit lawn,
Eats the beetles
Till the dawn.

Drains the daisies
Of their dew,
Sleeps by day
In an old black shoe.

Reggie Hedgehog
You have chosen
In our tiny lawn
To stay.

You may chase
The big black beetles,
Till the sun
Disturbs your play.

Slugs

It's very wet outside,
Slugs slip out
Like brown ships seen from the air
Stretching armadas across the path.

I bomb them with blue pellets
And later kick their wreckage,
Still and spare,
Into the lawn's edges,
They sink without trail or trace.

I sleep now. To dream.
Of horns gorging,
Greedy deaths,
Sluggish despair.

Frog Boys

Halting by the wood-side's paint-still lake
Cut off from the trickling rain-spent fall,
The water surface almost seems like land,
Solid enough to step upon you'd think,
But in that muddy water, close at hand,
Little blobs like brown eyes blink.

Standing to stare and pondering
'Look at those, I think they're frogs!'
The peace is cracked by noise, a wandering
Gang of boys, with jam-jars, nets, and dogs.

We leave them to their foolish play,
Putting frogs in jars and letting others go.

Glad to see them happy in their day
(But sad they took the frogs away).

Warwick

A crocodile of children winds
Round the narrow edge of walk,

On pilgrimage to the ancient keep,
Where dungeons, tortures and weapons of war
Will less disturb their eager talk
Than that tiny guttered dog,
Sprawled too stiff and log-like
To resemble sleep.

Mole

By the wall
Where hard earth begins

The mole is dead
Lost in the act of digging.

His shovel-like hands
Are red

His tiny blind eyes
Are closed.

All stiff and tight
His velvet head,
The tip of his nose upturned.

He fought the good fight
When he was alive,

And this is all he earned.

Loss

Where are you, little squirrel?
Lost in the woods?
I hope you are not too lonely among the trees.

Here it is sad without you,
And up among the branches and the leaves
I look for you each day,
But find you only in my dreams.

Little Brown Dog

Little brown dog
Lost in the street,
How you hate the unfriendly
Feet and noise.

You hurry from pillar to post
With your stumpy tail,
And your worried small face
(I wouldn't like to be in your place).

Little brown dog
Lost in the street,
Where will you go
When it's night?

Will you sleep all alone
Without your bone,
And dream of the days
That were bright?

Little brown dog
Lost in the street,
I wish I could help you home,
But I have to go now
For night's coming on,
And I must leave you alone.

Lion in the Zoo

His bars divide him from the world
People point at him and laugh,
He'd like to claw them limb from limb
Or bite them neatly right in half.

For LIFE he lingers in the cage,
His mane is mouldy with despair,
All day each day he stalks in rage,
Throws his blunt claws in the air.

Next week, next month, next year, he'll stay,
Locked in the lair he never chose,
With wire and steel and bits of shade,
And keepers dressed in shabby clothes.

For EVER in his iron cage,
His lion rage is penned in tight,
For EVER in his lion skin,
His lion soul knows no delight.

No wonder that he's getting thin
And suffers bad dreams every night.

Wild Flower

Dearest little wild flower,
Into what corner of what field
Has the wind blown you?
Searching I have not found you,
Though I remember like pain
Your beauty,
Your perfume in the air,
Your presence everywhere.
Dearest little wild flower
Shall I see you in the spring,
Or will winter hide you,
Like a child, shivering?
Yes, I know you are there,
Lost in the high woods,
Or at the meadows edge,
Safe from harm,
A gentle sun warming you.
And when we walk
Down familiar lanes
I shall find you, know you,
Touch your face again.
For ever
The love of my little wild flower
Remains, remains, remains.

Poor Tiger

Tears trickle down my tiger face,
My whiskers twitch all out of place.
I think of jungles long ago.
Hunting plodding buffalo,
Birdsong in the Indian heat,
Taste of honey soft and sweet.
Monsoon rains and times of drought,
Rich harvests or when food ran out.
Days of joy and times of youth,
Healthy then in limb and tooth,
Sleek of fur and fast of pace,
First and foremost in the race.
These days my claws are wearing thin,
Fights become more difficult to win,
And every sadness strikes me down
Striped in colours like a clown.
I think of splendours in the wild
When I was just a tiger child.
Then I grew and learned things new,
Travelled forests through and through.
Now I languish in a zoo
Thinking of things I used to do.
Tears trickle down my tiger face,
My whiskers twitch all out of place.

Hawk

Suspended as from thread
A hawk hangs high,
Puppet of instinct or desire.

Now, hawk, hurl
Down,
Hurtle on the prey,

Before your great arms tire.

Bird Garden

Flame-blue parrots shriek
Or beak to beak joust,
The Arctic owls blink, blink,
A wide-eyed exile,
And the great brown owl,
Large as a log,
Like a man on the night-shift
Starts and winks in sleep,
His dead yellow chicks
In the pink dish wait for night.

Flamingos bend their knees
Backwards in lapping weeds,
Macaws carouse in curse,
Toucans take fright, and
A flame-red parrot large as a kite
Roosts tropically in the gnarled tree.

Frog

Somewhere down there
Our frog lives in the drain,
And if you turn the water tap above
So that it sounds and seems like rain
Within a drop or two he'll startle out
Like an old man from his house.

And as it runs some more and more
Our frog is beaten back again,
And when the wet begins to pour
He's flung like flotsam down the drain,
And from his flooding open door
He swims his limbs but makes no gain.

Until the human hand upon the tap
Turns off the flow and tides thin out,
And then a pause, and then his eye,
Blunt, questioning, with shoulders bent,
Peers through to look with grim intent
Still half surprised and still unsure,
To watch the wet turn into dry.

Stoat

Snared by steel
The young stoat's guts
Cling to barbs of wire
That clutch and cut.

Sweet rotted fur
Where many winds
With tufted wool
And crow's flesh swing.

Among sharp teeth
And feet well shod
This, like Esau,
Sought his food.

One dusk in grassy gloom,
Sneaking to an egg,
A trap smacked rusty jaws
On the white leg.

So one sick pelt
They flung on a hanging row,
To perch with pigeons
And the spent crow.

Bullocks

A rusted saw sings sharp
In seasoned wood,
Its warping cough brings
Cattle to the wall.

By blackberried hedges
A blind man edges
On his usual patrol.

When wood is out,
Hard-sleek in sheaves,
Bullocks shift their ground
Towards a line of lane.

They lift dumb heads
To see a stick tap sound,
To where his darkness leads.

Spider

Near the door
A damp patch.

Beyond the stain
Of half-forgotten rain,
In the no-man's land
A small island.

You with your spidery flight
Pilot the little canopy.

You cannot hope for much respite
No more than a fly.

Never mind,
Tonight it is wet outside,
But your little legs are dry.

Giant

Alone inside my ugly cave
I crave with all my cavernous heart
The love of princess or of knave
But linger here apart.

They fear my wrath and evil mood,
My clumsy feet, my giant size,
So now I cook my lonely food
And listen to their distant cries.

Once I was young and dreadfully proud,
Running like a tiger through the land,
Pulled up forests, bellowed loud,
Patted mountains with my hand.

Now I stay at home all day,
Listen to the wolves at night,
The young giants wander out to play
(I have grown too old to fight).

Too stiff and grey
Too stiff and cold,

My giant bones
Too huge and old.

Frog in the Grass

Squishy little frog
Moving in the grass by night,
You gave me a fright
I nearly trod on you.

By the light of the stars
I can just see you,
Your legs push like a swimmer
Towards shelter.

You are a true frog,
Not as big as a toad.

I would like to comfort you
In the palm of my hand,
But I don't dare.
You would leap too much,
Squirm and tickle or
Squirt horrible messy stuff.

As you hurry along
Your eyes look
Fearful and bright,
The load of your body
Too much for legs to bear.
You'd rather be in a pond,
Or the stream by the field,
Eating insects by the hour,
Anywhere but here.

Giraffes

Giraffes are funny long-legged things,
Sometimes in their striped jerseys
They run faster than footballers,
Or stand still and stiff like kings.
They hold their heads high,
Eat leaves in huge trees,
Or nibble candyfloss on low clouds.
They pretend not to see things go by.

Giraffes are enormously proud,
They hate to be disturbed,
Preferring to be elegant and sedate,
Their voices are not very loud.
Giraffes are never impolite
(They don't like the bully-boy lions),
They would rather keep to themselves,
And have seldom been known to fight.

Giraffes could never be cuddled or stroked
In their dappled pyjama suits.
They don't need our affection,
They prefer not to be laughed at or poked.
They just want to be left all alone
In the hot African day
(When people photograph them
They turn their faces away).
So if you see a giraffe
(Perhaps escaped from the zoo)
Pretend you haven't seen him
And he'll do the same for you.

Escaped Budgerigar

There through the window
On the overgrown path,
Near the blackberry bush with its bristling fruit,
Where the lawn gleams green,

A flash of yellow, a crooked beak,
A little bird among the stones.

Sentinel in the apple trees,
Sit thrush and sparrows,
Somewhere a magpie clears its throat.
Over rooftops pigeons swoop,
Two gulls like vultures float.

Open the door,
Call him,
Catch him,
Or say something.

Perhaps he belongs to a child who cries,
Or to an old lady who taught him to speak.

Open the door gently
Go before he flies

But at touch of door
Or step on path,
The magpie laughs,
Sparrows flit,
Thrush trills an angry call.

The bird with crooked beak
Wheels and flees,
Yellow firework
Against trees,
A flying flower.

Off in a streak of light he flows,
Past bushes,
Brambles,
Tree tops,

He goes!
He goes!

Daddy-long-legs

Daddy-long-legs flying into the brightness,
Why does the electric lamp lure you?

You will get your long legs crumpled
And your frail wings rumpled,
And we'll never straighten you out.

Ah, you have flown from the lamp.
You rest on the sitting room wall
Like a sliver of a jewel.

How beautiful your slim limbs,
Your silver gem-like wings.
I will cup you in my hands gently
And take you to the door.

So in the evening light
Once more take flight.

There you go, flying low,
Then up to the soaring height.

Take care, daddy-long-legs,
With your long legs in the night.

Poor Bull

He stamps the ground
Like a lord,
Wears his crown of horns
Like a king,
Rules the unseemly herd.

Soon he's brought low,
Taken, prisoner-like, to town.

Where he'll wear a rich gown of blood
Till the sword cuts him down.

Bull

My enemies are deadly
And they wait
In coloured rows
Behind the gate.

With my poor sight
I cannot see the foe,
But when I smell them
Then I go.

My horns I sharpen
In the air,
On shapes of bodies
Hardly there,
Or heave my weight
At nameless things,
At blood-red butterflies
With stings.

Bitter,
In my fear marooned,
I stamp the ground,
I feel strange wounds.

I rush and toss
At flimsy men,
Who step aside
And stab again.

I taste sick blood
Rise in my throat,
Sharp darts and daggers
Strike my back,
My front legs stumble
And I slack.

Heavy with feeling
On darkening sand,
On feeble knees
I hardly stand.

I run great rivers
Where their weapons stung,
I breathe where steel
Has thrust and clung.

And as in pain
To sleep I fall,
They cheer my death
Beyond the wall.

Plovers

Close by nettled hedges
Plovers search,
Snatch insects from green stubble.

Now that machines have scythed
The shrew and rabbit's refuge,
Birds usefully peruse
Summer's leavings.

Crested heads
Like tiny sharks,
Glean leather jackets
Till the ravaged fields
Edge with dark.

Bear

I am a tiny little bear,
Lost on an ice floe
Somewhere, somewhere.

As I pass the North Pole
Over there,
Does anybody care, anybody care?

I float on by
Quite in despair,
Going nowhere, nowhere.

I am a tiny little bear,
Lost on an ice floe
Somewhere, somewhere.

Bird with a Broken Wing

Bird with a broken wing,
You stagger round the lawn
Looking for bread and worms,
Poor little lop-sided thing.

All your friends desert you,
Pecking at your feathers,
Jostling you for crumbs.
Whatever will you do?

Perhaps a cat will catch you
As you limp under the bush,
An angry tom or hungry tabby
Hearing you blunder along.

I would like to help you,
Nurse you in a silver cage,
Full of moist seed and milk,
And put your wing in a wooden splint.

But it would never work,
You fear us far more than the cat,
And never like to be caught.
You prefer to take your chance.

Bird with a broken wing,
You have no hope to fly,
The earth is hard and unkind.
You will hunt for food till you die.

A Camel with a Honey-Coloured Hump

Once I knew a camel
With a honey-coloured hump,
He ran across the desert
With a hop, a skip, a jump.
His eyes were brown and lazy
His legs were swift and slim,
Throughout the whole Sahara
No one ran as fast as him.

The pride of all Arabia,
The joy of all the land
The honey-coloured camel raced
Across the honeyed sand.

In all the desert places
They knew him by renown,
The fastest camel ever
In his coat of honey-brown.

If you ever see a camel
With a honey-coloured hump,
Who runs across the desert
With a hop, a skip, a jump,
Whose eyes are brown and lazy,
Whose legs are swift and slim,
If he's running quick as lightning,
It must, it must be HIM!

Nostalgia

Come back sweet pterodactyl
And sing to us awhile,
I miss your wings and tiny feet,
I miss your little smile.

I know we never knew you,
A million years ago,
But though you upped and left us,
We love you even so.

Seasons and Months

Seasons return, and today I am fifty-five
And this time last year I was fifty-four
And this time next year I shall be sixty-two.
HENRY REED (1914–1986)

Spring

In early April,
Holy Week,
I become quiet.

Rain laps at windows.
Light settles water-coloured on trees.

Spurts of dark
Spill over me.

Green spring winds
Push at windows,
Laburnum flicks its hair.

Starlings peck anxiously
At their soaked potato on the lawn.

My face at the window
Makes them move,

Rising like hopes.

Sonnet

Now showers have loaded every stalk
To sloping fields along the muddy lane,
New from winter barns the quiet cows walk
To feed on grass and hedges once again.

Some days before the apple-blossom burst alive,
Moved into sound with song of thrush and bees,
Now hurriedly before more rain the insects drive
From flower to flower among the coloured trees.

Inside my house a freckled window-pane is spun
With many tiny spiders come to birth,
They cross warmed glass together to forestall the sun,
Touched into gentle movement like the earth.

But of all spring's images this most imagination fills,
Behind the farm a black bull feasts on yellow daffodils.

April Snow

Skies thicken, sudden blue
To graveyard grey.

Momentarily old,
Grass, flowers, children, trees,
Freeze before they grow.

Holderness Spring

Now garden paths
are dressed in pink,
frail blobs of blossom
torn from trees
by yesterday's rain.

Today blackbirds again
patrol the lawn,
casting cautious eye.

And on the broken fence
two doves sing, and look
as if they're loving spring.

May

Among red may a speckled thrush
Fills blossom, sky, and bush
With sound, so much so his song
That starlings like school boys rush
To perch along a branch
And mock his round.

In sprays of laburnum sparrows
Launch from twig to twig,
Incessant in the evergreen,
To visit nests with beaks of fluff.

Forget-me-knots are spread
On paths like blue flung stars,
A thousand pretty weeds.

In a vacant plot dancing dandelions
Shiver away silver seeds.

Summer End

In the half-dark
I can smell the roses
After rain.

Each wind-swept petal
Tipped with wet,
Their rose-velvet skin
And thorny stems
Lifted high as a man's head.

I thought of what
The gardener said,
How each long flourishing
Flower would soon be
Pruned, cut back again,

Till green plaintive
Stumps shiver
In the rain.

Autumn

The fading sun
Elongates behind browning trees.
Each year this season
Strikes with its chilly shock,
And the body ages
Under the blows of a blunt sun.
Mind cannot repair its summer loss.

Oh fading sun,
Bringer of day and night,
You are the dream in flight.

Fall

I am the ripe pear
Ready for the grass below,
I wait
And do not wish to go.

All summer through
I grew and grew
Along the bough.
And autumn will remove us now.

Hanging fruit on trees
Luminous in dusk,
The dying sun sadly touches each with light,
Full fruit or fallen husk.

September End

Autumn's surge
Dulls far fields.

Against rain arrows
A horse turns tail.

Green is grey-masked
By a dead sun,
Mind is shadow cast,
Mist enters the heart's fire.

Bereaved of summer
Skin pouts bare against
Autumn's sudden fall.

Somewhere beneath wet roots
Creatures flush hard earth,
And prepare for sleep.

We too could sleep,
Absorbed in dream.
Instead through rain's torment,
Bent on walking,
We pace uneasy feet
Through autumn's turning.

Autumn Trees

Rain is spoiling the pears,
Falling on the sensitive skin.

Where wasps once walked
Water enters in.

The Winds of Autumn

Is that why the winds of autumn blow,
To shake the trees and make the apples grow?

Oh, that it was so, but no –
The winds puff, huff, and blow
To tell the swallows it's time to go.

Autumn Leaves

If you came to my garden now
You could be Queen of the Leaves,
Your subjects dancing at your feet,
Trees waving arms in the breeze.

The old man walking his dog
Would not believe what he sees,
Children hurrying from school
Would linger for hours like bees.

But best of all would be banquets at night
When after the venison, capon, and trout,
Fireworks flower over the trees,
Till the moon was wreathed in silver smoke,
And everything would please.

If you came to my garden now
You could be Queen of the Leaves,
Your subjects dancing at your feet,
Trees waving arms in the breeze.

After the October Storm

After the storm
Sunlight seeps
Across the lawn,

And the wind softly weeps
Through the big tree's thinning leaves.

Birds in frantic, frightened flight
Rush back and forth like bats
Against the yellow light.

October

Harsh rains spill spent thistle,
Striking dead nettles.

Leaves in red-clay clusters,
Shape like hands
Over black-sodden soil.

Fog

Houses like desolate ships swim,
Floating heavy
In dark wool.

Eaten roads
Lead to the mist's belly,
Ghostly children drift beyond roses.

Season-broken, burned-blood leaves
Bury chill shattered gardens.

Like lost people
Trees signal and drift.

Poem for October

Winds whip arched tree-limbs
Bare as if they'd shift
Bark not only leaves.

Already hedges gored by machines,
Their heads steel-gashed,
Show scarred bark.

Dead-fleshed in white scab
Ruined hawthorn,
Twigs prickled as hedgehogs,
Shrubs wounded
Weeks before winter.

The Weaver Hills

On lines of hills the sun
Distinguishes skins of frost,
Ridges fleshed silver, green
Knots ice-marred, snow points
Glass-sharp in light-flecks,
Smoothed sheep-fields miles distant
Treeless like the moon.

Lines arched in chill,
Land splitting a cool sky,
Dune-crusted, cloud cluttered,
Wintered by west winds, sharply
A cleared skyline sweeps clean,
Ice-capped the high ground lies.

Ice

If breath could melt the world
We'd breathe upon the ice
Until it melted, changing iron iciness
To soft liquid white running
Towards the sun's heat.

But now black ice flows down the hill
And where the sun lifts slowly above
Petrified houses, people walk puppet-like,
Children cautiously slide, a dog madly
Skids over the ice-skin.

December

Ice points wink,
Crisp on graves.

At sea men choke in ice,
Their ships broken to waste steel.

Here the town's shovels
Clear paths for postmen red-faced,

Children bob down
Innocent sun-touched glaciers.

Snow

Cold white horses
Graze on milky grass.

In this dusk
They are sculpted from snow,
Rooted in dark
They cannot go.

Cold white horses
Graze on milky grass.

Winter's End

The wild dogs of winter
Start to retreat,
Snapping ice-white teeth
At dead trees (rain plummets
From an evil sky).

This is the cusp, crust
Of divides, splitting
Dark winter from spring light.

Long is the cold night, weight of
Wolf bears down, the pack runs
Free in the unleafed wood, their
Dog-masks growling for food, slouch
Away they will but now the going
Is hang-dog, as slow as their approach.

Bric-a-brac and Ragbag

I must lie down where all ladders start
In the foul rag and bone shop of the heart.
THE CIRCUS ANIMALS' DESERTION
W B YEATS (1865–1939)

Scarecrow

O scarecrow,
Little symbol of sorrow and pain,
We need you to drive the birds
Back into the air, our bluff and shield.

Because we all have to feed,
So we stood you there,
Tramp-like,
Directing traffic in the middle of a field,
Crucified, with crumpled hair.

Omens

A wolf peeps in
Through the window,
And my computer
Is malfunctioning.

The moon burns
Its strange light
Through space,
Stars fall through
The vacuum.

Strange

It is a strange wood here,
Strange in entering,
Strange in the finding
Of winding paths
Where birds cease to sing.

I am at a loss.
All maps lost.
And for these thickets
No plans suffice to wrestle with them,
Meeting each green ambush,
Wetland or pool,
Rich with indifferent wildlife.

Worse still is night.
Slow sunsets torment
Those high green arches,
Till darkness shadows and frightens,
Creatures scuff in the growth.

Hurrying I trip over roots,
Tentacles of foliage joust and snare.
In thick dark I taste blood.

We cannot sleep here.
Pursued by darkness
May dawn hurry.

Running

Over stones, past
Tree-limbs wind-stripped,
Race, pant against pulse,
Beat heart fast, hard.

Woods become body, as if
Falling down moss and slope,
Limbs leap at space, each
Flesh-particle, blood,
And filament of thought
Strain, stress to movement,
Distance speeds apart.

In the frost-driven park
Whatever electric pulse moves
Hard bones and soft flesh into
This dance, is lost to circling
Birds, wet grass, thrusting
Branches, and the solitary
Dawn runner racing against the wet
Winter sun.

Hong Kong

In this dark heat my friend, the fan,
Looks left and right,
And left and right again.
Throughout the night
His friendly stare
Throws on my body
Heaps of air,
A fragrant blowing to and fro
In Cyclopean sentry-go,
To warn off enemies of heat and sleep
Which for my tender flesh compete.
Hot, cool, hot, cool,
He waves his face
To cover all degrees of place.
He breathes to every corner here,
Sighing gently in his arc,
Spreading spring-like waves of air
As through the open windows come
The torrid breezes of the east.
And as they fall into his zone
He tells us that the cool is best
And still maintains his monotone
And with his plaintive contoured face
And filigree of silver lace,
His lullaby sends sleep to all
Who under his soft rhythms fall.

And till the morning's waking light
He proves all faithful through the night.

Doors

O the mind, mind has mountains…
—G M HOPKINS

Inside the mind are many doors,
Each needs a special kind of opening.
Some to be flung open, thrust back.
As boys run through doors,
Others to be gently ajar and quietly nun-like to
    be moved.

Some fly open in the wild winds
In getting to know the house,
But barred and bolted doors
(Some from inside, some from out),
Are the ones worth finding,
Leading on to other doors,
Doors up, or up and down stairs,
Doors into cellars, attics, dungeons, spires, (no end
    to these),
More doors at ends of corridors.

On either side another floor, another level,
More always more, door after door.
'I never knew the house was this big!'

When winter comes or habit creeps like damp up walls
People like to huddle in a single room,
Never opening in or out for themselves or visitors,

The rust corrodes, dust fills in arcs where doors
    should open,
The handle turns stiff, better not to disturb,
But open doors swing through space,
'And there's another one!'

And opening into winter may remind of spring,
Opening doors,
One less to open,
One less closing.

Trapeze

Life,
That intrepid trapeze
From which we hang,
Dangling man,
Or swing up and back

Or fall,
Crack,
To the slack net,

And the crowd roars.

Time's Reflections

And Time, a maniac scattering dust,
And life a Fury, slinging flame.
IN MEMORIAM, CANTO 50
ALFRED LORD TENNYSON (1809–1892)

Serving Time

That dog, marooned
In the iron kennel
With fearsome leash
And yellow teeth,
Yaps all night long
At imaginary burglars,
And in the morning licks
His master's hand.

That boy, confined
In the dusty room,
Scribbles inkily
And is bullied
Unmercifully,
And in a later year
Endows his misery
With the nostalgic ear.

That man secured
In offices for life,
Dust in his nostrils
Anguish in his heart,
Accepts his engraved clock
At the appointed hour
There where his life ran out.

Summertime

Thirty-six summers spin hot
Over my head, the sun glares
Angrily into yellow gardens,
The blue blares into unshaded eyes,
Only flies have energy,
They circle dynamic as worlds,
And in some eternal distance
A jet streams white-tailed into space.

Here in fusion of tree, grass,
And squawking bird, against the
Hot ground, eyes half-closed into heat,
Where the lids orange.

Images of fish, still
In a glass pond, or of arms
Metamorphosed into trees,
Or of a single unicorn cut clean
Into a green hill, burn in the eye.

Love's Time

Love lames and enlivens time,
Spills it wantonly
Like jugs of petals,
Or hangs time
In still air,
A large cut tree
About to fall
But not falling.

Love's heat
Dissolves dials,
Melts clocks.

Where love scalds
Time's simple measure
Only is love's pulse.

Decisions

Still just time to decide
Which rivers to cross,
Which horses to ride.

And look, the late afternoon sun
Already starts the downward slide.

Time's Silence

Time moves,
Never looks
To what was
Or might have been.

Its voice is silence,
Or almost so.

You hear it
In a deserted library,
At sea or in space,
Or see, as in a mirror,
Each changing face.

Tiger Time

Time is the untamed tiger
Who eats us in the end,
When young we sport together,
He seems to be our friend.

Later, longer in the tooth,
We walk with him each day,
But his tiger's claws are soon unleashed
And he'll wound us all the way.

Time is the untamed tiger
Who'll watch and stalk and wait,
Once out of his familiar lair
He'll no longer hesitate.

Time is the untamed tiger
We still thought was a friend,
But his appetite gets bigger
And he'll eat us in the end.

Sunt lacrimae rerum

'I weep for all things human.'

That short distance between
Wholeness, nothingness,
Our span, grasp,
Small under the stars.

Thirsty in deserts,
The crying child,
The top spinning
Till it stops.

All that is past
Or will come to pass,
And pass,
All we hoped for.

And that silence
Beyond.

Dusk

Quiet sad day
Crawl to your end,
A faltering butterfly
Waving wet wings,
We cannot save
Such wasted things.

So sleep now
Till turning day brings
Another space,
And morning comes
And the early thrush sings.

Timing

Clocks inside my head run slow,
I think I'm younger than I am,
But climbing boys on coloured trees
Correct the elements of sham.

Now it's almost winter here,
Not quite (but almost) and it's coming on.
Days drift like leaves, and in my head
Dogs howl for hours against the sun.

Time, Gentlemen, Please

Drifting at night in the car's comfort
I see the young returning from dances,
And in a season of discontent,
Having had mine, I envy them their chances,
Their golden showers, their glossy greenest grass,
(I chafe against time of fast and Lent,
Thinking in research of all lost time that went).

How absorbed they are, the couples
Fooling drunkenly round midnight takeaways,
Lounging in the brightest nightlife gaze.

I look through the smeared-ice windscreen of
   perpetual greys,
Grey hair, grey days, greyness is all, that silver spent,
The horse put out to graze, the old grey mare beyond
   the fence.

I have survived to prove a simple thing upon the
   drum-like pulse,
That time moves on and having moved is not the same.
For once upon a time intensity froze all things on
   the move,
Held all in frame, the laughing eyes, the lips, the hair,
The round-the-corner careless lack of care.

Now time removes the quickness and the game,
It's serious everywhere.

If only one could seek return
To that kingdom of the younger self,
Could we not grasp the seconds in our hands like snow
And feel the melting moments ease and grow,
And in the place where things have faded fast,
Find a substance that might hold and last?

As always, yes and no –
Yes, as from that melting newer streams would flow
Yet in that swift current, time would still dissolve
   and go.

So let the young return from dances now
They'll find out anyhow,

Returning from dances late
Only makes time hesitate.

Visit

(For John Bradley)

We came
To see you
In the closeness of time,
Towards the closure of time.

You were thin as a clock,
Morphined against pain,
Changed from that month past
When you and they
Knew less.

So difficult to talk
The small change of time.

We drift in the afternoon sun.

Through thick closed glass
We glance at the early summer grass.

Till it is time to go.

Playtime

Children know no time
With their innocent skipping.

Only instant intent,
That minute, that moment.

Under blue skies and
Scattered buttercups.

Characters

*What is character but the determination of
    incident?*
*What is incident but the illustration of
    character?*
                      PARTIAL PORTRAITS (1888)
                      HENRY JAMES (1843–1916)

Widow

Years of harvest are gone,
Autumn aches on.

For the lonely
Love is not done.

Far from the sun
She picks up
Lost ears of grain.

One by one
Tasting the years again.

Friday

At five she leaves the bank,
Her silken hank of long blond hair
A blatant promise
In a world of wilderness.

Tonight her golden tresses
And seductive dress,
Will be undone.

That's when her stallion
Comes on with tender word,
To sheathe his magic sword
In the scabbard of her flesh.

(Oh consummation
Devoutly to be wished!)
His sweet behest
Is never to be missed
And she will not desist.

Afterwards, amid the peerless night,
As he smokes and takes a well-earned rest,
She'll muse on all the useless days and months.
Whispering to the moon's smile,
"Yes, this was the best,
This was the very best."

———

The Fight

Inside the cat's cradle of the ring
I sling my leathered stones,

Goliath feints and flings
Them too…

I draw blood,
So does he.

In a flood
Of mutual blows
Each knows
What the other knows,

Piling the heap
Of pain on pain,

Till a lucky gain
Rocks him or me
To sleep.

The Boxer

Slumped in the dressing room,
After the fight, eyes sore,
My head a broken bloom,
Red tulip lips, blood on my tongue,
Ears singing as if a hundred bees had stung.

What has been done
I can't recall.
Only the rain of blows
On my china chin, a vague counting,
Silence in the hall, and here I am,
After the fall.

Old Jim, smiling, comes in,
And shuts the door,
Keeping out the raffish pack
Of those who always come.
I sit dejected, speechless,
But he pats me on the back.

"Sorry, mate," I whisper
through painful teeth.
He looks surprised, confused.

"I can't remember!" I say,
"No need," he says, "You did damn well,
I don't know how you made that second bell!"

"Screw that!" I say, "I let you down,
Myself, and Molly too, and Fred!"
I feel huge tears swell in my eyes,
Trickling down my cheeks like fire,
I'm so ashamed, I hang my head,
Like some poor dog that did the dirt.
(Inside and out I hurt.)

"Don't be like that, my son," says Jim
(A strange look coming on),
"He knocked you down till kingdom come,
But you got up and landed one,

He went down like the setting sun,
He bloody lost – you won!"

First Love

He gave it to me straight,
I gave it to him straight.

He laid me on the floor,
No one had come inside before.

Not much in it,
A few minutes.

Not love, not much to share.
As if I'd lost something
Not knowing where.

Things were different then,
But not quite.

I went home.
Cried all bloody night.

Slaughter Man

To him all fall prey,
Pig, goat, lamb, calf,
Bull or ancient horse.

He discovers day by day
Secrets of the animal self,
Smells blood and primal force.

Evening time he goes his way,
Greets his children with a laugh,
Eating covers his meat in sauce.

The Torturer Goes Home to his Children

Daddy, daddy
It's been a long day,
And we've been to school
And there's games to play.

And we fell over in the playground,
See, and bruised the skin,
And we learned all kinds of things
About history and sin.

And the teachers frowned
And kept us in,
Daddy, daddy
It's been a long day.
Daddy, daddy,
Tomorrow please don't work,
It's All Saints Day.
We could go to the sea
Or sit on daddy's knee
After we've been to church.
Then down on the beach
We could sample a peach,
Tasting the tasty juice,
Before we dive and swim, and swim
In the racing waves.

Thinking only of you and us
(And forgetting *him*).

Spinster

She caressed the tigers of the past
Till they purred and purred.

Loitering, like an iris fading
In a forgotten country, she grew old.

Until memories mellowed and at last
She told her sister's children of
Her younger past.

Teacher

We who are fated
To spend hours together,
Best years of your lives,
Many of mine,
Why should we fight
Cornering each other?
Why should any of you
Hide deep in the herd
Or shiver in silence?

Your lives and mine
Meet in this instance,
As we clash and lash at each other,
Or open a tedious book,
Or shrink to oblivion,
Or shimmer like fish on a hook.

Sheltering like shells
In the colony of lessons,
Emerge from your patterns
Of noise or stillness.

Together we could strive
Into knowledge like crabs
Exploring the sea's edge.

Train Journey

Green trilby, dirty overcoat,
That wild beard, jutting, husky brown,
Gives the game away.

He spends the journey
Telling anxious ladies
"The toilet lock does not work."

Explaining, demonstrating,
Checking, telling,
His constant moving opens
And closes sliding doors.

Trapped we listen
To his overloud voice,
Those explanations,
Time after time.

Trapped in his concerns,
Never noticing ours.

Wedding

They run the gauntlet down the aisle
Where two sides wait on his and hers,

Contrary armies ranked in file,
Those regiments of saboteurs.

The bride's demeanour under fire
Of snipers aiming at her face,

Hides all banners of desire
Beneath a mask of scalloped lace.

He walks erect like soldier blue,
Advancing elegant and slim,

Patrolling through an avenue
Confused by thoughts of her and him.

Her mother suffocates a sob
(She finds it so hard not to weep).

Imagines that yob on the job,
Surrenders to the salt-stained deep.

The wail of hymns drowns out the sound
Of rustling tissues, flushing tears.

The vicar's voice on sacred ground
Drives forth the coward's quaking fears.

The deed soon done, new treaties signed,
From the vestry the combatants emerge,

To beat retreat through trenches lined
With armies waiting for the surge.

The flash of camera guns declare,
A battle won, some battles lost,

As girls cavort and young men swear,
And daddy calculates the cost.

Judge

The attics of my mind are crammed with law
As red-robed, wigged, I ride to court.

Safe in my limousine with armoured door,
Riders fore and aft protect the fort.

From judge's house to courtroom we career,
My learned friends smile softly and agree,

Into my goldfish bowl outsiders peer,
I smile and nod my head with dignity.

It's good for all to glimpse me here,
Guardian of the values of this land,

Glassed in, unreachable, remote,
But visible, theatrical and grand.

We go at speed, on silver wheels we glide,
The chauffeur's brief is quicker than the law,

The law's delay will never here abide,
But danger lurks in every moment more.

Before diurnal labours can begin
In quiet comfort I enjoy my ride,

But in the mind's uneasy lingering
I often think of those I put inside.

Within my covered and most learned head
Exist cruel images of legality,

Caged men, those cohorts of the living dead,
The clanging gates of jail, mortality.

My sentences, my juries, and my fines,
All quaint majesty of power,

And in my hand a golden pen soon signs
Away the years that stretch and sour.

At home, in limousine or court,
I do not forget what I must do,

Judge, justice of all earthly law,
Custodian of the human zoo.

Rider

Cowboy complexion,
Dark eyes under the brow,

Hard hairy hands, big fists,
A rider's walk.

His element the prairie night,
Under stars where the herd stands.

When he buys you a drink he insists,
Do not interrupt his talk.

Legends like halos follow his head,
A killing or two, the usual jail,

Somewhere in his past a special woman,
And many fine horses.

Gardener

Bent double an old gardener grubs for weeds,
Under his green fingers straight sentry
Rows of crops push up through dry soil.

He knows quaint names of flowers as neighbours,
Squats like a child to pluck radishes,
Sniffs close summer air as if blossom,
Eyes the weather, rich in comment.

New shoots of onions bristle from the dust,
Lettuces like green shells swarm the earth,
Potato orchards crowd against a fallow plot.

Copsed in green against a line of farms,
Under the birds' artillery of sound,
He digs with strong brown arms.

Cooped in by nettles where the remnants are tossed,
His smile is like a crack in clean bark.

Dancer

Free in the dance's swing
She slings her limbs,

Her flimsy skirt flirts space
In circles of sweet guile.

Rings of spilled energy
Wrinkle her face almost to smile,

Under a canopy's furl
A patch of sky-white thigh.

Within a snaky curl
She shivers her woman's shape,

Sharper that dance's arc,
Quicker her pulse's shake.

So in sensuous centrifuge
Soul and body snare like one,

Spun as a top towards dream
She treads steps to swan-like oblivion.

Faster that gait's swift whirl,
Feet castanet like hail,

Tenser the dancer's painted face
Under her music's veil.

Book Shop

The man's a wheeler-dealer in his hat,
Up and down ladders looking for Spain,
So high his cloth cap touched that
Part of the ceiling he said leaked rain.

Then down like a whippet and outside the door,
Along to the second home of many books,
Scattered like broken thoughts upon the floor,
Torn leaves in darkness where no one looks.

But the best is to come, across the market place
He leads us in Pied Piper's eager dance,
Unlocking doors, upstairs (he points), we face
A million books, all scattered, left to chance.

We pay our debt, the haggling done,
We carry a bag of books from chaos to the sun.

Fairy Tales

Ich Weiss nicht was soll es bedeuten,
Dass ich so traurig bin,
Ein Märchen aus alten Zeiten,
Das kommt mir nich aus dem Sinn.

I don't know why I am so sad,
I cannot get out of my head
a fairy-tale of olden times.

DIE LORELEI
HEINRICH HEINE (1797–1856)

Princess

Oh Princess,
When you go to sleep
Sprinkle star and moon dust
On your eyes,
So you may dream
Of palaces, gardens, ice cream,
Happy walks in the park,
Birthday surprise.

Oh Princess,
Do not fear the dark,
Even when,
Beyond the palace gate,
Wild wolves bark.

Safe inside your cosy bed,
On the pillow lay your golden head,
And dream all night of lovely days
And precious things,
Sea haze, butterflies' wings,
Meadows where the tame bird sings,
Tasty fruit, smiles, and precious rings.

Till all the bad things go away,
Until the sunlight touches you
At break of day.

Woods

Just before night
The friendly woods
Go gaunt and black,
Trees hold up large hands,
Go back, go back.

And over little woody trails
A dark owl hoots and glides
And wails.

By day the green
Gave shelter from the too-hot sun,
Now over tripping roots
We cannot run.

We are not wanted here,
Not wanted here,
Dank moulds of wood and leaf
Squat near.

Now friendly woods
Grow shadows black
And full of fear,
Trees whisper words
Go back, go back.

Song of the Fireflies

We are born at dawn
When the soft light comes,
We will dance
All day in the sun.

We will dance in the sun
Till our wings are strong,
We will dance at dusk
By the riverside.

We will die
When the cold dew
Brushes our wings,
(Brushes our wings),
We shall die
By the light of the moon.

And the new fireflies
Little sisters, little brothers,
Will dance in the early dawn.

Destinies

As flies to wanton boys, are we to the gods;
They kill us for their sport.
KING LEAR, ACT 4, SC. 1, L.36
WILLIAM SHAKESPEARE (1564–1616)

Song of the Hanged Man

Lost under a dwindling sky
I dance endlessly.

Caught by the rope's sharp eye
I shape quaint choreography.

In my little ring I dance
Every watcher stands entranced.

As still as statues in their space
Each turns an eager living face.

Till lighter are my urgings grown,
No dance pulses from the heart,

And in a skyless world alone
I hang untended and apart.

No poor puppet now will tread
Towards that earth our bodies share,

To something nameless and unsaid
My dance is broken in the air.

Salmon

Swim
In spring
Up long rivers.

Yes,
We do too
Till tides
Turn

And the suck
Of the sea
Plucks us
From our will.

War Trilogy

Boy Soldier

    I am the soldier
    Born to bleed.
    How is it
    That this uniform of skin
    Is so soon enclosed
    In an ulterior form?

    Not long
    Flung from the womb,
    Into the battle's mesh, my
    Mother's blood on this
    Pale flesh not dry in
    Time, my face like hers
    Still soft and smooth,

    Along the trench of death I curse,
    And into history's tyrant gaze
    I bite on the unpalatable grape.

March-past

Khaki unfolds itself into such
Splendid snakes.

Faceless tunics, polished boots and
Men marching through the streets.

With such a sound of tinkling brass
And sounding cymbal,
Tinkling brass and cymbal sounding shall
Resound, tinkling brass sounding cymbal
Shall resound,
'Among the guests star-scattered
On the grass,'
Shall resound against the green rag
Of the ground, that brassiness
Of brass and cymbal sounding.

And women must weep
If not for death,
Then for love.

Photo of a Dead Soldier in a Middle Eastern War

Eagerly his mother
Watched his early walking,
Each tentative balance,
A steadying touch.

In his eagerness
He rushed into the spiral spin,
The dying fall.

A handkerchief marks
Where his face was,
His boots flung out
Like still planets,
His hands as brown
As dead hares.

In Memoriam

(Dave Cooper, saxophonist)

They all went different ways
Young as they were
Sinking whisky-sodden to the gradual grave,
Or choking, eyes bulging, on the office floor,
Or yielding to the sudden scalpel probing the
    open skull.

Only the first had famous last words, things like
"I'm pissed off with all this," and "Sod it all,"

That little old gent of forty, chemically bald,
With strange squeaky hoarse voice, who,
Two fingers to the world, blew music hard to the end,
His saxophone wriggling like a snake,
Long wringing lines of sorrow, his signing off
    swan-song,
His message on life's border, "This is the beauty
    I learned
And all that I know," pared to the bone that sound,
Indelible on the smoke-filled air, saying it.

City Dweller

I'd like to be,
Sometimes,
A shepherd or a sailor,
Locked, enclosed,
Like a piece of a jig-saw puzzle
Into his own particular
Part of nature,
That lump of hill,
This square of ocean.

A share of city streets
Gives each
Bodily space
To parade or stop,
But there's small
Distinction in it.

To rub shoulders with valley or
Horizon, the brisk
Wind or sun slashing
The flesh, to crave
No other,
That may be best.

Occasional Poems and Elegies

And the stately ships go on
To their haven under the hill;
But O for the touch of a vanished hand,
And the sound of as voice that is still.

ALFRED

ALFRED, LORD TENNYSON (1809–92)

Trumpeter

(For Dick Hawdon)

More times than I can say
I heard you play,
Now time has slipped along
And changed your song.

So we change too
From what we were,
Or thought we knew
Or understood,
Remembering
Your bright seasons
Of harvests full and good.

Now we must hold on,
Like children in the dark
To what we know.

Such magical times
Down busy years,
The golden rivers of sound
You shaped and found
As in a dream or visions of dreams past,
That which echoes on in soul and heart.

The song which does not leave us,
Though the dear singer must depart.

Remembering

(For Robert Spencer, lutenist)

After life's long joy and suffering
The lute lies untuned,
Its strings untaut,
The tablatures unread.

It's semper dolens, semper darkness now.
Through each heavy night
Comes not sleep but thought,
The mind's discord,
Resonances of disquiet.

Sweet memory,
Lay not your hand
Too heavy on the heart,
For he now fallen asleep
Strove to remember
Those who touched us deeply
With dissonances of shadows and unrequited love,
Exalting their lutes aloft like banners
Before they left the stage.

From centuries
We weep their tears,
Speak their words,
And in our souls
Their songs still rage.

Yes, he remembered them,
Put on new strings,
Tuned their lute,
Traced messages
From the inky page.

So much becomes
A new remembering,
Of them and him
And all they had to say.

For us in restless beds,
Haunted by song,
Come, heavy day.

But while we stay awake
We remember too,
Them and you,
As together you sleep on.

Dear Jack

(For John W Duarte, composer, critic, teacher.)

You left us in a time of sorrow,
Your going was another burden in a heavy year
When time (so many times) had leaned down
And whispered in our ear,
And we, drained dry of all but feeling,
Turned again, this time to mourn your passing.
Accustomed as we were
In the dying weeks of that year
To hear the long bell tones of sadness,
The sudden silence beating on the brain
And slow regret for loved faces disappeared,
Now shocked again beyond words we were
To realise another loss,
The long perspectives of your life lost,
Our little worlds crushed into strange winter shapes,
Your music in a moment moved into posterity.
Sleep after bad news breeds its own nightmares,
Waking into that dark dawn is a fitful dream,
And caught between darkness and darkness
Where night and winter day join hands,
What is there to say or think but sadness,
And rehearse lines of memory like tired tunes?
When light full breaks after days of semi-dusk,
Cloud smothered and all sunlight lost,
Then sense returns, we are here, you are there,
And we remember how brave you were,
And how you always seemed to tell us to be brave,
Flourishing your pipe like a sword.

Perhaps we should now be brave and try to restore
    our faith.
Difficult, but out of the dark, memories come,
We think of other moments past,
In the day's heat, the brightest light,
Of what we had, not what we lost,
And what you won for us in life's long fight.
And so we turn to some immortal part,
A touch of melody, a happy harmony,
Some words upon a page,
Or something spoken and well-remembered,
Some moment when you handed us your heart,
Some quite unintended sweet memorial,
Silver notes sung by a silver lake.
And as you settle down to sleep,
We'll hear the music of your dreams,
Attentive to things we missed before,
Seeing things we loved, more than before,
Listening to the heart within the voice,
Listening to the pulse within the heart.

And though the traveller rests,
Who knows how the journey goes on,
And though the singer departs,
We do not forget his song.

Retirement Party

This little ceremony of goodbye
Is rather strange, it shouldn't be,

I've seen so many standing here,
Glasses raised, with heart-felt phrase,
Enjoying the banter and the cheers,
Surely I should have learned by now,
What ought and what should not be said.
(Like words mouthed from a moving train
Or the wave from a departing ship).

So searching for proper words to say
I scan through voices and faces of the past,
Not many last to memory, life is too busy here to
    remember ghosts.

I remember bitter-sweet emotion
From those who somehow stumbled
On the best ways to bid goodbye,
I remember bitterness from others,
Those who said they did, but didn't really want to go.

I remember reminiscences, anecdotes, we already
Knew and know.
I remember bits of this and that,
Yet most of what they said,
When it comes to it, I forgot.

But now my moment's come to face the test
And add my litany to the rest,
The ideal farewell-goodbye address, borrowed
    from those
Who went before, a rehash of familiar prose,
So, hold tight, handkerchief ready,
Here goes!

Dear Colleagues, this little ceremony is rather strange.
(It shouldn't be).
In years to come I will remember you. (Some of you may
Sometimes remember me).
We spent much time together,
Sharing the rough and the smooth, the highs and the lows,
    the smiles, the storms, the jokes, the blows.

I wish you the best of luck for the future. You may
Need it more than me. I am staying at home in
My quiet harbour, while you put out to sea.
So goodbye, my dear colleagues,
And a fond farewell
From me.

This little ceremony of goodbye is strange,
Just as I thought it might be.

Guitarist

(For Brendan McCormack)

Of late we'd heard of various sad departures
With further rumours on the wind,
But your leaving, this cannot be true,
We do not believe what ears receive,
Words spoken have broken substance,
Mortal things deceive.

Truth to tell, we have indeed been told,
The Pied Piper has left town,
Mercury's wit silenced.

Off-stage the guitar is no longer tuned,
Ah, sweet remembered sounds of voice and string,
You liked straight tunes well played.

We listen in vain,
And in this cruel spring sun, we know
Orpheus has died before Eurydice,
And the fallen bird no longer sings.

Royal Wedding

It is a time of happiness, no doubt,
Not just for them – the favoured few,
But also for the common herd who view
As through a stained glass window
Whatever comes and goes.

Mounted guard, limousines, cheering crowds,
The waving flags, we see it all,
And in our hearts we seek a kind of certitude,
A reassurance we are vibrant and alive,
And through seeing visions of delight
We rejoice within the human hive.

The day has come for us to savour secret dreams,
Images of wish-fulfilment and desire,
We watch the triple union of birth, wealth, and fame,
And see the kindling of love's sacred fire.

We wish we could move closer to the flame,
And yet the old illusions hold,
In some strange way we feel we know the pair,
And on this day their lives we share
In a personal way, as if we all were there.

We watch the screen intently as the play unfolds,
The flickering emotions on her lovely face,
The bridegroom's arm slipped round her slender waist,
How sweet, how normal, how sensitive they are,
Reminding us of other weddings, and the way we were.

Once they are married and have sealed their fate,
They move off to whatever feasts and palaces await,
Only a fool would not wish them well, the very best,
Fine children, long life, happiness, and all the rest.

Epithalamion

(For Kate and Andrew Liepins)

Dear two
Standing there
As never before,

Our hearts
Stripped of all but feeling,

And you, the groom,
Your voice, strong and proud,

And you, the bride,
Your voice, a tiny sigh,

The warm afternoon
Moist on our cheek.

Now it is complete,
We drink your smiles like wine
And walk on angel feet.

Moments

I've had my moments, I will confess...
(POPULAR SONG OF THE 1930S),
GUS KAHN AND WALTER DONALDSON

Remembrance

Your love for me was like a thousand flowers
Whose bloom in summer soothes the beating heart,
My love for you was like a child's sweet dream,
Together then and never more to part.

My love for you was like the highest tree
Which reaches to an infinite sky,
Your love for me was like the deepest sea
Where passionate waves build high.

My love for you was like that secret gold
Within the rainbow's magic sight,
Your love for me was like a lovely story told,
By Shakespeare's sweethearts on a moonlit night.

Parting

Foolish to think
As if written in stone

She remembers
That day.

But for me, left alone,
Were things to say:

"How can I live without you?"
(December branches drip with grief)

"What are we doing?
Your leaving is beyond belief."

To the Music Lesson

I watched you as you walked
Down the long road, in a hurry,
Your feet moving with purpose.

And you were lost to the world,
Your head wrapped in music
As if in armour,
As if the trees sang,
As if the clouds spilled sound,
As if the pavement trembled with chords.

For now you are a bird
Hurrying to the dawn chorus,
A singer hastening to the choir,
You will play like an angel.

You will return
As full of music
As a sack of magic blackbirds,
All singing together.

Quarrel

A day of bitterness and curse,
For she in her mood
Clawed at my heart.

Till I burst into anger apart
And tore her in two
And we fought
Like dogs in the park.

I walked out to the lonely street
In indignant retreat,

To seek by the sea
Peace in the softness of waves,

Away from the tide of her tears
(Though they ran through sand and surf).

Patio

Impatiens, busy Lizzie,
(Crimson blood across the earth)
Has drunk deep from the storm,
Clematis, summer carmine,
Let elegant petals fall.

But look, snapdragons
In their finest gowns
Dance like girls
Against the wall.

Garden

She has dressed her garden like a poem,
Where every flower has a part to play,
Though the summer drought has scorched them,
They fly their colours every day.
She knows them all by name and loves them,
And hates it if a flower dies,
They sometimes wilt like humans in the heat,
And droop their lovely heads and close their eyes.
Shoulder to shoulder they stand proud,
The crowd of flowers clustered one by one,
Their variegated colours distinct and loud,
The best ones stand like soldiers in the sun.
So many flock to seize attention,
Lilies, cornflowers, hollyhocks and others,
Crocosmia, pinks, hydrangias and delphiniums,
Lupins, red hot pokers, proud like brothers.
And then there's pansies, begonias, iris, and
    sweet marigold,
As well as lavender, carnations, and roses (best of all),
They lift their tiny faces to the sprinkling water can,
And drink and drink from the blessed water-fall.
Like us they will sleep deep when winter comes,
Some of them may shiver and die,
She'll miss the ones that take their leave,
And whisper a fond goodbye.
She has dressed her garden like a poem,
Where every flower has a part to play,
Though the summer drought has scorched them,
They fly their colours every day.

Round Midnight

Early – the world's my oyster
(Later cry stinking fish),
In the morning my sun is rising
(By evening the old death wish).

At dawn my gull is soaring
(At dusk the Icarus fall),
First light it seemed like everything
(By nightfall nothing at all).

Words

Swift as an arrow
That thing best unsaid
Sped to take root in flesh.

Can it be taken back?
Dug from the wound?

But never.

Judas in his dying fall
Remembers this for ever.

The Dream

Yes, it was a dream, where I called your name
Into the wild wind and round the edges of the sea,
I was calling you, you were calling me.
And then, like Orpheus with Eurydice,
I lost all substance, utterly,
Swept from your company…

Confused I woke with gasping start
Into the day's nightmare, lonely and apart.

Roof

(Homage to Robert Frost)

On the membranes of a flat roof,
A magpie or a boy retrieving a ball.

Feet scrunch on the pebbled flat,
Scuffling, a heavy rustling scratch.

Must be a boy, some urchin scrambling,
I must leave my work and shout.

Unlock the back door,
Into the garden's bracing air, round to the roof.

But opening doors disturb the bird,
I see it fly up like a machine.

Where it scampered all is flat and clean,
Devoid of boy or bird.

I would prefer to see it on the roof
Whatever intruder it was,
With boys I could have words,
With a magpie admire,
Watch for its mate.
Now birds and boys of reality or imagination
    have flown,
I regret I was noisy and too late.

Riding

Re-making myself to his rhythm
Bianco canters,
Irons ripple like bells,
A monk bends to his garden.

But for us it is the field,
Their manes shake,
The horses dance,
Who can hold them now?
We fly at space,
The wind spins in our ears.
Flanked by the electric fence
We charge the hill,
To left and right
They pass,
Urging on.
He and I
Chase them
Into the sun.
Till wildness and fury
Subside,
The firm turf
Rests.

Then towards home
We gently ride.

Letter

Forgive me friend
That I have not written.

The months have gone by
Like a cat's sleep
Before the fire.

Evolution

My life is a fossil
Possessing its natural resistance,
Pressed down upon
By forces beyond itself.

In a million years
A mad geologist
Might find embedded in rock
The shape of my soul.

Round like an ammonite,
Curved like a seashell,
And in the middle
A jagged hole.

What caused those contours?
At what depth was it found?
It was not buried deep
In chalky ground.

It came from an age
When souls were often lost.

River Suite

Moon

    We stood together
    To see the moon swim
    Across a dark river.

    Perhaps never to return
    But if I did
    Always in this place
    Will be your shadow
    Watching the moon's face.

    On that day
    When you hear of my death
    Think of that light on the dark river
    And the silence beneath.

Storm

    You left me to face the thunder alone,
    Racing through the rain
    Like an escaped dream.

    I sit with a sad beer
    While rain falls
    Like blessing on my skin.

    Somewhere in the thick rain
    You are running like a deer,
    I am here
    And you are there.

Mountain Walk

Sometimes the sun caught you in its glance
Through shade of green and branch
On the steep path, suddenly.

Into sharp light you came
Smiling from your labyrinth of looking,
Finding flowers, shells, berries,
Pods to be shaken near the ear;
Such treasure there.

And in the walking hours
I drank your smiles like wine,
Glass after glass.

Flower

Tonight a single star hung there
Touched your hair like a jewel.

Walking through the warm streets
You picked a flower to share,

Thoughts

Wine sings a song
Fresh bread tingles the tongue.

Soft light falls on rivers,
Our moon is a poem.

Beyond

As from a distance seen we wave,
Where once we watched together.

Now rivers run between.
And only in a wish or dream
Will you be there.

And where I am,
Rivers will whisper your name.

Ending

Moon and sun
Go and come
Rivers carry on.

You are there
I am here.

But who am I,
And who are you,
And when,
And where?

Memento

How sad the holiday photographs
With their silent laughter,
Blue skies, blue seas,
Hot sun into the lens,
For ever after.

Endless unfocused waves,
Or here a pyramid or two,
Nearby a camel struts
With awkward rider,
And another feeds.

Like Egyptian kings
Caught for ever in frieze
For us too time recedes.

And after precious lovely days
On tinted prints
The light begins to fade.

The Look of Love

I thought I saw love in your eyes
But found I looked in vain,
Your lovely gaze was just surprise
Like sunlight seen through rain.

I thought I saw love in your eyes
You whispered I was wrong,
How foolish of me to surmise
The singer was the song.

I thought I saw love in your eyes
Like fruit upon a tree,
But golden apples tantalise
To ripen fancy free.

I thought I saw love in your eyes
Though you did not agree,
That light of love I realise
Was love that came from me.

I thought I saw love in your eyes
But found I looked in vain,
Your lovely gaze was just surprise
Like sunlight seen through rain.

Night

The moon swings
Soft as a woman's face.

Stars like silver spiders
Spin light.

I think of you
Worlds away from this place,

Wiping frost from your eyes,
A taste of snow on your mouth.

Absence

oh
darling, the skies grow grey
when you are unhappy,
the winter sun weighs heavy,

you have
gone out and I listen for
your hand at the door,
your
light tread in the hall.

oh come
back soon, sweet flower,
the hours grow long without you,
and I wish
to look at you and hold your hand,

and we
can talk of happy things,

or weep
inwardly together
at the
world's folly.

Reflections

A Cartel of Poets

Dangerously tight-lipped
Living by a secret code,

When the sun dips
They leave tear-stained poems,
Like broken flowers on the road.

Lorca

In the square they frighten children
Near the church they shoot men
Upstairs in the hotel
They hurt the women again.

Blood-tinted the wheat-fields
Bandaged the limbs of trees
Valleys reek with breath of guns
And hum with stinging bees.

Silent is that poet
His mouth full of blood
In taverns not far
They joke over wine and food.

The Inward World

(For Malcolm Williamson)

In his country a sharp light
Blazes – long journeys of sound
Return and turn – on bright
Coasts enormous waves ground
On vibrating grain, stone or soul,
Incessant their song.

Here like perpetual noon the twelve
Bells of music pound life-long.

Shouts tear the inner citadel,
A spent bull kneels, spills again.

In his land alone he dreams of pity
Where Orphic horses sing to men.

Poem for Hilary Comeau, artist

Lines trapped into shape,
Sharply in movement,
Spear against the eye's
Observances, colour assumes
Velocity at the wall's stasis.
Landscape spontaneous
With vision, shifts
In the mind's refraction,
Endowed towards being,
Consigned to the eye's keeping.

At the speed of light
Jagged brilliances
Splay to the room's softness
His disturbances of seeing.

Elsewhere a quiet thistle
Or sculptured relics of trees
Twist towards abstract
His imaginings' taking of shape;
Created from the experiment
Of their selves unstill
They hang animated.

This man's seeing
Selects, things
Natural to his taking,
Shape as wood or stone
Sensations into making.

Rock-obsessed, texture moves
To solidity, on surfaces
Canvassed, a natural sculpture
Tends to depth, colour-evoked.

Shaded into activity
Levels of tone control
His vision's inclinations.

Retrospective Exhibition

These corridors
Say
In their echoes
When, when,
And again.

And we
Remember
When and when,
Again.

That young
Boy waits.
Yesterday
He was at the gate.
Now, a young man, he passes on,
Stepping on stones
Over the shallow river.

Now it is late
And a grey man
Gravitates
From one state
To another,
Till there is no other.

The lover,
Silent in his soul,
Picks flowers
From his lady's garden.

Now is he whole,
And summer buzzes
Busy in the hedges.

Over your shoulder
See that priceless picture,
And another,
And many more,
Stretched along the gallery
Like jewels on a necklace.

Before each frame
Stand back, consider,
Read the artist's name.

Rain

Poets are enticed to rain like bees to flowers,
Evoking images for all their lovely whims,
From Keats's subtle 'weeping cloud' to showers
Of 'sweet refreshing rain' in harvest hymns.
Or Lear's Fool railing at 'rain-water out o'door',
The 'bellyful' that so confused the old king's brain,
He stayed too long in 'rain, wind, thunder, fire' and saw
Drenched steeples, drowning cocks, till utterly insane.
Kind farmer Robert Frost beseeched the southwest gale
To 'Come with rain' and 'find the brown beneath
    the white',
He knew a thing or two of melting snow or hail,
And when the inner and the outer meld just right.
Eliot's sad April stirred 'Dull roots with spring rain',
Remote from Chaucer's naively cute eruption,
When 'Aprille' with his 'shoures' bathed every vein
In 'swich licour', breeding 'vertu' not corruption.
'Still falls the rain' for Dame Sitwell, 'black as our loss',
Meant bombs, nails, hammers, and the Field of Blood,
Not innocent watery stuff but Christ and Cross,
Après moi le deluge, that nightmare Noah's flood.
At school we read with passion, *Il pleure dans mon coeur*
Comme il pleut sur la ville:
'Boys – homework – take this down –
Translation of Verlaine for tomorrow!'
Oh Sir!
It pees in my heart like it pees down on the town!

Things are Not the Same

I must tear up my poems today
Letter by letter, word by word,
Let not a single syllable be heard,
It is time to put them away.

I read them as if from a different year,
Some of them are fine,
(The occasional pleasant line,
Like music on the ear).

But these feelings give me pain,
I was a clown in the circus of devotion
(Though my love for you will remain).

But things are not the same,
How could they be?
I am no longer me,
I must change my name.

I must tear up my poems today
Letter by letter, word by word,
Let not a single syllable be heard,
It is time to put them away.

Books I've Never Read

Those books I've never read
That have escaped,

Like people one could have known
But never did.

What have I lost?
Oh, worlds of experiences,
Words tossed away
Planets unexplored…

I miss you all,
I yearn for you,
I am sorry not to be with you…

Please forgive me,
Sweet neglected pages,

My fault
Entirely.
I shall look for you
From now on,
And perhaps find
What I should be looking for…
Or perhaps not.

Violin

That Swedish fiddler
With his rhythmic head
Legs akimbo, tapping foot,
Speaks with his bow
And tells of cabins
Deep in snow,
Or sings of roots of ice
Long lost in forests,
Or the frozen lake
Beneath whose skin
Spring currents move deep,
As they do in him.

Poetry

Dear friend,
We spoke of poetry, did we not?
Bringing to mind so much.
Such words divide.

For each heart-felt leaf
I ever threw at your feet
Met only damning silence.

So what passes between us
Is little enough.
We plough different fields
Opposite harvests.

Pity it is
For words fall then
Like autumn apples
That cannot be eaten.

We are lost for words,
Worlds apart, birds in separate cages
Hanging dark.

So let it be,
And so let's talk instead
Small or politics or dirty.

Anything but poetry.

On the Occasion of Antigoni Goni's Guitar Recital

(At Mikulov, Czech Republic)

No longer our Antigone
In some alien town,
Rather now another
(Hitherto unknown, hidden),
Dreaming of Greek tales,
Singing rivers of silver,
Kissing the sleeping muse of Paraguay…

Till our hands close and speak –
Do not return
To your cloudy mountain.
Stay with us.

But look,
As echoes, like shadows,
Tease the ear,
The plinth where she sang
Is empty.

(Sadly we wake from the dream.)

Guitar

Sing, golden girl
With your Arabic mouth,
Sing of your long history,
Sing of what you have seen.
Sing, golden girl
Of half-forgotten things,
You who will never be old,
You who have seen so much.

Sing, golden girl,
Of when you were young,
You are the colour of the Spanish sun,
You smell of forests
And sweet-scented trees,
Sing, golden girl
Of nights long hidden
Of dead lovers, of assignments
On Moorish balconies.

Sing, golden girl,
Sometimes with restraint,
Often with wild sobbing
Like an abandoned child.
Re-awaken memory,
Draw from dry souls
Some wild desire,
Till blood runs fresh in rivers,
And we become
What we truly are.

Sing, golden girl,
With your Arabic lips,
Sing for the man who loves you,
Your flesh reflecting the light.
Sing, golden girl
Of nights long past,
Of dead lovers, of the mystery
Of Moorish places.

Sing, golden girl.
Your voice trembles
On the edge of deep silence,
Or murmurs water-like,
Or hums like a hive of bees.

Sing, golden girl,
Speak of the eternal city,
Tell us of our immortal home
Wistful, unsoiled, ideal,
That which we would be
And would become.
Sing, golden girl

The Grand Piano

The GRAND PIANO! A remarkable creature,
So elegant, so polished in every feature,
From the sinuous contours of its figure
(With its eminent dorsal, up or down)
To its three slim legs and pedal-jigger,
The GRAND PIANO whether 'baby' or bigger,
Really is the most fashionable beast in town.

With its keeper's kindly coaxing it opens its teeth
    and sings,
But if tormented by boys (please, please, take note)
It mumbles miserably from that cavernous throat.

Though usually now well-tempered, suitable for
    polite society,
Soirées, concerts, or more frivolous flings,
For the connoisseur it will oh so delicately shiver
    its strings,
And unforgettably
Declaim a variety of marvellous things.

Humour or Otherwise

Humour is odd, grotesque, and wild,
Only by affectation spoiled,
'Tis never by invention got,
Men have it when they know it not.

To Mr Delany
Jonathan Swift

Pride

A youth stood upon a wall,
The youth was small,
The wall was tall.

Pride comes before a fall,
His friend pushed him,
That is all.

Song of the Drunk

I'm not as jober as a sudge
Neither am I a shrunken drine,
I'm not yet as nissed as a pewt
On martini and wine.

Of whisky I had just a tipsy
So I'm feeling fine,
But I'm getting tightly slipsy
On martini and wine.

The bunch powl seemed exciting
And the sherry was divine,
But I'll stick to metting gerry
On martini and wine.

I've never felt so happy
Since I was nenty twine,
When I fell in love with whatsher name
On martini and wine.

And then she went and left me
For a dirty swotten rine,
And I'm left to drink for ever
Martini and wine.

Hitler

Hitler
When naked
Probably
Looked
Not very different
From Mister Aitch

Who
Also
Has
A moustache
And lives
On
The parish boundary.

But
Clothed
It becomes
Comparatively
Easy
To
Tell
Them
Apart.

Banana Skin

Is there a banana
In that banana skin,
Or has all the banana
Been taken out,
So there's no banana
Left in?

No, there is truly
A banana inside
Its own banana skin,
So the banana is not without,
It is indeed within.

Well, leaving it there
Is a sin,
I shall take it out
And eat it.

And though the banana skin
Will then be incomplete,
I shall be entirely replete,
With a banana
Within.

Girl in a Red Hat

"My coat is black,
The street is grey,
My hat is red."

Walking along,
It's as if she said,

"Are you all looking at me
In my red hat?
My red hat
Is well worth looking at.
And to look at my red hat
Is to look at me."

Yes, to left and right,,
Observe that turn of a head,
To see
A black coat
In a grey street
And a red hat.

It's as if she said,
"My red hat and me
Are well worth
Looking at!"

The Chair

(Homage to Samuel Beckett)

I suppose I could sit here for ever
And never move from this chair,
But if I sat here for ever,
I'd never get anywhere.

I suppose I could sit here for always
And never move from this chair,
But if I sat here for always,
I'd always be sitting there.

Good Intentions

Mister John J Johns
Saw a girl
Drowning
In white rapids.

So stripping
Off all his clothes
He dived
In
Naked
Hairy
Among
Foaming water.

He rescued
No less than
Three girls
All naked,
And
A dog all hairy

Before being arrested
For indecent exposure,
And
Other
Offences.

Poll Tax

(For Margaret Thatcher)

I am the little man, pole-axed, poll-taxed and vatted,
By every springtime fiscal wisp of wind that blows,
My silver poll is duly counted, added, swatted
By that strange strategy a politician knows
(And in my middle years the damage shows).
I am the money-maker, fraught, caught and courted,
Pursued down endless avenues of forms,
My private matters declared, reported, sorted
In line with laid-down bureaucratic norms
(Each gentle season breeds its own specific swarms).
I am the money-giver, leased, fleeced and bereft,
Corralled by mortgages, demands and debt,
Each month assumes, illuminates, a kind of theft,
Wherein the hard-earned pittance shrinks more yet
(And what I have is never gross but nett).
I am the tax-payer, loaded, goaded, and controlled
By laws too subtle for the unaccounted brain,
Democratically persuaded, jaded and cajoled,
That my vote gravely can affect the gravy train
(Though often through the years I bear my cross in
    vain).
I am the citizen, denizen, rich venison of this land
Pragmatically, empirically, resigned to taxing fate,
Rendering to Caesar, (intending to please her with open
    hand),
All devious polecat polls ever to be levied on my pate,
('For lady you deserve this state, nor would I love at
    lower rate.')

Song

Where have all the good guys gone
The ones we loved when we were young?
Who sang the best songs under the sun,
Sailed cruel seas against the Hun,
Rode the range with loaded gun,
Filled the bad guys full of lead,
Played poker till their fingers bled,
Killed until the war was won?

They spoke from wirelesses (with a squeaky hum),
Smoked cigarettes while chewing gum,
Theirs was the world we loved and knew,
Theirs was the growing that we grew.

Where have all the good guys gone
The ones we loved when we were young?

Letter Poem

An insect looking for its T
Jumped upon U suddenly
(Smaller than a B
But a horrible thing 2 C!)
O dear U Z 1 8 it so
OK I Z it's 2 soon yet
4 U 2 panic or 2 fret
Y B afraid, it's not 2 bad
Its MT head is O so mad

Just bang it once and U will C
The little beast is R.I. P.

Reminiscence

(For John Betjeman)

Miss J. Hunter Dunn, Miss J. Hunter Dunn,
I cried when you died, aged just eighty-one,
It's game, set, and match, and close of the day,
And flags at half-mast down Aldershot way.

Now old men in Camberley mumble in grief
As they brush down their blazers and click their false
    teeth,
Lifting a tumbler of tonic and gin,
With quivering lip they remember sweet sin.

Miss Joan Hunter Dunn, what ineffable fun
To stay in the car when the dance had begun,
But what happened next I can scarcely recall,
Let alone what pictures you hung on the wall.

I asked you to be my dear blushing bride,
I can't bring to mind just what you replied,
But that doesn't matter, the pain still resides,
You broke our engagement and my heart besides.

Nursery Rhyme

Mary had a little lamb
Its fleece was white as snow,
And everywhere that Mary went
The lamb was sure to go.

But Mary was a farmer's girl
As tough as girls can be,
And for that little bleating thing
She had no sympathy.

She took it to the abattoir
Where they cut its throat,
She joked to the jolly slaughter man
"That lamb sure got my goat!"

She put the pieces in a pot,
Gave the giblets to the cat,
And as for leg, breast, loin of lamb,
Mary ate all that!

Performance Poems for Children

*Et, Ô ces voix d'enfants chantant dans la
coupole!*

Parsifal
Paul Verlaine (1844–96)

The Last of the Dinosaurs

How lonely to be the last
Lolloping dinosaur,
Long bodied lizard larger than a jumbo jet,
Without a mother or a mate,
Uncle or brother,
Alone on the cold primeval plains.

As the horrid ice-age began,
Just before the age of man,
All day long it was so cold
That dinosaurs died before they got old,
And their long tails froze,
And their huge bodies
Were covered with snow.

The last dinosaur to go
Had seen them all die,
And he was hungry and lonely,
And covered with frost,
And though he was as big as a block of flats,
He was sad and shy,
And totally lost.
He didn't know
At all what to do,
And there was no food to be had,
All the leaves of the forest were under the ice
And in that state didn't taste very nice.

And the great tree trunks of the time
Had fallen down
And were covered in slime,
Beaten down by the wind and the ice.

How lonely to be the last
Lolloping dinosaur,
Long bodied lizard larger than a jumbo jet,
Without a mother or a mate,
Uncle or brother,
Alone on the cold primeval plains.

The Beginning

This is the song, this is the song,
This is the song of the dinosaurs,
This is the song, this is the song,
This is the song of the brontosaurus.

This is the song of the earth's beginning,
This is the song of the earth we are singing.
From the waters of the deep
Fleshy fish and slimy monsters
From the darkest waters creep.
Slowly up the sand they go,
Slowly up the slithering sand,
A thousand monsters from the sea
A hundred million years ago.
Up the sandy beach they creep,
Huge and slow.
This is the song of the pterodactyl,
This is the song of the mammoth beast,
This is the song of the ugly monsters
Crawling from the sea to feast.

Now they move towards the jungles,
Now they fly into the air,
Giant lizards wait like statues,
Smaller creatures make a lair.
All around the sound of eating
All around the noise of creeping
Moving, slithering, rushing, sleeping,
Animals, animals, everywhere.
This is the song of the earth's beginning.

This is the song of life and birth,
All around the world is waking,
Monsters through the jungle breaking,
Giants lurking, snakes jerking,
Tortoises waiting, tigers shaking,
Dinosaurs crashing, rhinoceroses lashing
Elephants smashing, brontosauruses bashing.

Noisier, noisier is the earth now,
Louder, louder, the sounds of life,
All are singing, the song of living,
All enjoying the earth's beginning.

This is the song of the earth we are singing
Singing, singing, singing.

King Canute

Wise King Canute went down to the sea
(Where big waves beat on that windy shore),
His courtiers all surrounding him there
Applauded and lauded him more
And more, and more, still more,
Till at last he could no longer
Adore their peons of unceasing praise.

His shaggy eyebrows high he raised
(H always did when his temper grew
And so they knew, and so they knew),
Canute had decided what to do
To end their disgraceful hullabaloo.

Shaking his kingly ancient head
One morning in the court he said,
"You praise me and flatter me,
And never desist, the time has now come
When I insist on showing you all that
Although I'm a king,
I really am not an omnipotent thing.
Come down to the shore this afternoon
When I shall explore extremely soon,
Just why I deplore your tedious tune
Of unceasing praise through all of my days."

So down to the beach the courtiers ran,
And when they assembled Canute began;

"Now if I'm as clever as you say I must be,
Which of you thinks I'm clever enough
To master the waves of the sea?"
(Right at this moment the tide's coming in,
The rain's blowing down and drenched to the skin
Those courtiers huddle to try and forget
Their fine clothes will ruin in weather and wet).

And yet when Canute proposes his question
As if with one voice they resist the suggestion
That his power's incomplete in the least degree,
"King, O, king!" they repeat,
"We all must agree
That you have the power
To master the sea,
Or make the four winds just cease to blow
Or make it rain
Or make it snow
Or make all the birds migrate to Spain
Or make them all come back again."

Old King Canute grows angrier still
But finally speaks to that shivering crowd
In his kingliest manner augustly loud.
"To show you fools how foolish you are
I'll order the sea right now to retire,
Something never envisaged before
Not even upon our English shore."

At once the wise king gave his command,
"O sea, advance not up the sand,
Canute, sole monarch of this land
Will make you obey his demand."

Closer now to the waves they waited
Until their shoes were saturated,
The tide crept up right over their toes,
Higher still higher the waters rose,
And quite soon wetness reached their knees
(One or two courtiers started to sneeze).

At last Canute laughed out for sport
(The waters high around his waist),
"Let's all go home," was his retort,
Their lesson learned to town they raced.

Where evermore the talk is told
Of how Canute and his court caught cold.

The Plague of Frogs

One dark day in Egypt,
A long long while ago,
The Lord decided it was time
To smite the mighty Pharaoh.

Pharaoh hated Moses
And sniggered with a smile,
"No, no, no, no,
I'll never let your people go,
I'd rather throw them in the Nile
Or feed them to a crocodile,
I'll never never never never
Let your people go,

So there, so there, so there,
That's what you ought to know!"

Moses waved his magic wand,
Over the water, over the land,
Over the city, over the sand,
Over the palace, over the school,
Over the pond and the paddling pool,
Over house and over street,
Over desert, over wheat,
Over the goats and over the kids,
Over the parks and the Pyramids,
Over the kitchens, over the sinks,
Over the statues and the Sphinx,
Over the roofs and over the stones,

———

Over rocks and over bones,
Over the rubbish and over the bins,
Over the boxes and over the tins,
Over the big things, over the small,
Over the short and over the tall.

Down came every plague we know,
Plagues of ice and plagues of snow,
Plagues of lice and plagues of blood,
Plagues of drought and plagues of flood,
Plagues of toils and plagues of boils,
Plagues of cats and plagues of dogs,
But worst of all came plagues and plagues of
Frogs! Frogs, frogs, frogs,
FROGS!

So Pharaoh summoned Moses and said,
"This is no joke, this is no joke,
The whole of my fair Egypt
Has turned into a croak.
I hate their froggy bodies,
I hate their bulging eyes,
I hate their silly hopping,
I hate their tiny size.
I don't mind plagues of locusts,
I don't mind plagues of mice,
But a plague of noisy croaking frogs –
It's really not quite nice;
They leave frogspawn on my carpet,
And puddles on the floor,
My dear sweet Mr. Moses,
Please don't send any more."

Moses pondered deeply,
Then turned to him and muttered,
"Esteemed and ancient Pharaoh,
The words that you have uttered
Show true and right repentance,
Which pleases me to see,
And with every word you've spoken
I heartily agree.
With frogs this land is cluttered
From breakfast time till tea,
My people hate it also
As much as you or me.
So they have asked me if I'll take the frogs,
And cast them in the sea,
(Of frogs they're feeling very sore,
They cannot stand a minute more),
I'll have to move the frogs today,
Or else my people vow to stay
And me, their leader, disobey!
So now I say
Oh Frogs! Away! Away!
Thus I wave my magic wand,
And exorcise the dreadful curse,
But never mind, old Pharaoh,
I'll send you something worse,

And in the end, as you well know,
You'll have to let my people go!"

Daniel and the Lions

Down, down, down, down,
Went Daniel to the lion's den,
What a horrible dreadful thing
Just because Daniel annoyed the king.
And so, down, down, into the ground,
Deep into the dungeon's mouth.
Where in the terrible slimy dark
Wild dogs and wolves and jackals bark,
And behind the bars of the darkest cage
Hungry lions roar and rage.
Down, down, down, down,
Went Daniel to the lion's den,
How frightened he must have been then
Pushed into the cage by cruel men,
Without a single friendly face
To smile at him in that awful place.

The lions had frightening lion-like names
Majesty, Simba, Emperor, James,
Tamburlaine and Nero, Caesar and James,
Judah and Babylon, Simon and Tim,
All twelve were hungry and with eyes of flame
They licked their lips and looked at him.

Daniel on the lion's floor
Trembled at each lion's roar,
And in the flickering torch-light saw
The lines of teeth in each lion's jaw,
And heard the cruel laughter of the men
As they locked him in the pen,

And by reason of the king's own law
They rolled a mighty stone before the door,
To block out such a sordid sight
And keep him in there for the night,
Guarding him with bars and stones
(They'd come back later for the bones).
When the nasty men had gone
No wonder he began to moan,
And in a very plaintive tone
Begged the lions to let him be,
"Leave me alone, I mean no harm,
There is no cause for your alarm,
I love you lions, my name is Dan,
I really am a friendly man,
I love all creatures great and small,
I love all living animals,
I only wish you well and good,
Please do not take me for your food.
It is the king who keeps you here,
Darius the king who, full of fear,
Took you from your jungle home
Where you loved to stalk and roam,
He put you in the prison here,
Made you hungry, full of care,
Yes, oh lions, I love you well,
Let me share your humble cell,
Let me stroke your tawny manes,
You can ease my painful chains,
Let us sit around and talk,
Let us play and sing and walk,

If tonight you do not eat
Tomorrow may bring quite a treat,
God has made us man and beast,
Please delay your angry feast.
Let us trust in what He sends
Just tonight let us be friends."

Overcome by huge surprise
The lions blinked their big brown eyes,
Wondering this time what the king had sent,
They shuffled in embarrassment,
Not quite knowing what to do
In their tiny squalid zoo,
They looked towards their splendid leader,
Majesty (a massive feeder),
Who after just a moment's thought
In his deep lion's voice made this retort:

"Oh Daniel in this lion's den,
Do come and share our shabby pen,
Each of us in prison lies,
Distant from our native skies,
Here we linger day by day,
By friends forgotten, far away,
You are frightened, so are we,
Locked up for eternity,
You are gentle, kind, and sweet,
We shall lick your tired feet,
We shall soothe your troubled brow,
Hungry lions will guard you now,
You will ride upon our backs,
You will stroke our friendly noses,

You will sleep as safe as houses,
Till the morning call arouses.

In any case you're very thin,
Nothing more than lots of skin.
Your bones would taste like withered sticks,
Not the dish a lion picks,
It boils down to a simple question,
Are you good for our digestion?
Our answer then is very plain,
In sweetest safety do remain,
And when you leave, please come again
To comfort us in our despair,
We'll not make you the lions share!"

So all night long they sat and talked
And laughed and joked, and played and walked,
Dan learned to call them by their names.
He straightened out their tangled manes,
He brushed their tails and took out thorns,
He shook their paws and cured their corns,
He kissed their faces one by one,
And told them all that he had done
Until the rising of the sun.
And in the morning when the evil men
Came back to see the shambles in the pen,
They found not flesh and bones and bits
But on a pride of lions our Daniel sits,
So safe and sound; his gentle head
Had slept securely on the softest bed
Of lovely lion friends, all gathered round.

———

Sweet Tooth (or Tooth Suite)

There was never yet philosopher
That could endure the toothache patiently.

MUCH ADO ABOUT NOTHING,
ACT 5, SC. 1, L. 35
WILLIAM SHAKESPEARE (1564–1616)

Wish

    I wish that I was young and sweet
    Riding horses down the street,
    Clip-clop, clip-clop.

    Instead I am old and incomplete
    And as I walk my false teeth flop,
    Clip-clop, clip-clop.

Toothache

    Drained by pain
    I creep downstairs.
    My jaw hangs from
    The chandelier
    Like a tired horse.

Teeth

    My teeth
    (Live gravestones
    In the mouth)
    Loosen in the pull
    Of years.

    Time you old dentist
    Will you not stay
    To soothe
    The sweet smell
    Of decay?

Decay

Dentists from their private view,
Over years and tooth by tooth,
Move from the many to the few,
At last arriving at the truth.
My mouth is like a ruined church
Where once the choir in order stood,
But now a smile leaves in the lurch
Gaps which destroyed the brotherhood.
Of course when guests arrive for lunch
Wear your subtle plastic plate,
But when I settle down to munch
It hurts like hell to masticate.
Far better then to chew without
Than suffer such embarrassment,
The few survivors round about
Can bite enough for nourishment.
The jaw is our Achilles heel
(Don't look a gift-horse in the molars),
For long decades will gently steal
All substance from the alveolus.

Dentists from their private view,
Over years and tooth by tooth,
Move from the many to the few,
At last arriving at the truth.

Infirmity

I that in heill wes and gladnes
Am trublit now with gret seiknes
And feblit with infirmitie.
Timor mortis conturbat me.

WILLIAM DUNBAR (C.1465–C.1513)

Looking at You

(During her illness)

Looking at you
my heart is broken
Like ice
touched by the early sun.

Days pass,
stepping stones
over a dangerous river.

What is in our glass
we must drink.

Looking at you
my heart is broken.

Love

If love could make you walk
And bring you back to spring,
I'd fling flowers at your feet
And give you wings.

As it is, your pain remains,
And love flies to an empty sky,
I cannot heal a single hurt
Or cause a tear to dry.

The trial goes on, each hill is climbed,
Each footstep harder in the shoe,
And there's another range to go
Further than we knew.

If love could make you walk
And bring you back to spring,
I'd fling flowers at your feet
And give you wings.

More than Ever

I love you more than ever every day,
The way you look at me melts my heart,
And when you take my hand my life has wings,
I love you more than ever every day.

I love you more than ever every day,
I love to hear the things you say,
I love your silences and the way you look at flowers.

I love you more than ever every day,
To be with you is to walk a golden way,
With you is the only place I want to stay,
I love you more than ever every day.

I love you more than ever every day,
And all the weeks and months and years that pass,
And the more we love the more we may,
I love you more than ever every day.

Chest Clinic

Doctors grow wise
Before their time,
It comes from all they have done,
Studying anatomy and other ologies,
Seeing babies and old ladies die,
While we were having fun.
Now she sits before me,
A young Indian sage,
On the wall the x-ray of my chest displayed,
Ribs east to west apart,
Those prehistoric wings
(Not a photo where I look my best,
Thoracic zone, lungs and things).
So measured, weighed,
Blood pressured, pulsed,
Next she listens to my heart,
Stethoscope cold on the breast,
Tapping the xylophone spine,
Observing the respiration out and in,
And all the rest.
Back at her desk
Ominously she writes,
Asks idly,
'What kind of musician are you?'
Strange request, one is tempted to reply,
"Good enough, I hope!"

But here plain fact is best,
(It all goes in the book!)
(Awaiting x-ray the whale man
Baseball capped, wheel-chaired, tattooed,
Coughed stones and intimated slime,
Choking half-way between hyena
And emetic lion,
While I malinger with a magazine.)

So putting down her pen, a little pout,
A human gesture to dilute doubt,
'Nothing to worry about or fear,
Just further tests even if your
S-O-B (shortage of breath – apnoea)
In certain chests
Prognosticates a kind of death!
Fix a further appointment on your way out.'

Somehow it brought back when
Aged ten I saw the lovely sights
Of the distant town
From the tallest tree in the park,
And my father's shout
Barked like a dog below from the green dark.
'Get down before you fall!'

And I, who knew no fear climbed down,
For ever after frightened of heights.

Hospital

A score of visitors
Clutch flowers and fruit,
Talk hushed as if in church,
Stare at laughing nurses
Skipping down noisy stairs.

Some quip from a man alone
(Quite old, he's been here before)
Brings a laugh from women
Huddling round the closed door.

The door is opened,
Pinned back, secure,
Past so many beds the mobs disperse.
A patient starts to cry,
Another gives the wan grin of the old,
Others call out endlessly for nurse.

The visitors swoop on spare chairs,
Pull them to the space between each bed,
They give their gifts and sing like birds
Till everything they have to say is said.

Final Approach

Statistically it may be affirmed
The rest comes relatively soon
(Though perhaps no cause
For immediate alarm).

We feel its symptoms
In the breast (heart and chest),
Ageing legs, aching arm,
Spasms in stomach or face.

Just a phase (the doctor says)
Just this,
A weariness of days.

And while in certain ways
We don't give a damn,
It's you and I we'll miss.

Homeward Path

This week a shadow joined us
On the homeward path.

Entering the house
From the homeward path
The shadow settled in,
Taking over the hearth
As if it owned our earth.

A miracle may not
Come to pass it seems.
Having trod the homeward path
We share its dreams,
Its tears, its bitter laugh, its wrath.

After Her Illness

At whistling in the dark
None so assured as us.

And round the perimeter
New trees have grown
New skins of bark.

New wolves are also there
The forest beckons in.

The pity of it all
Is that the way home
Paths through the pitchy park
Where shadows roam.

A Lake Called Panic

We live near a lake called Panic
(Waters deep as the sea),
Few know it quite as well as
You and me.
We live near a lake called Panic
(A wilderness of our own),
Spend every day there
You and I alone.
We live near a lake called Panic
(Often cold and sad),
Some days are dreadful
Others aren't so bad.
We live near a lake called Panic
(Its waves sing like a curse),
Some days are bad prose,
Others just bad verse.
We live near a lake called Panic
(Close by a town named Tear),
Might as well get used to it
Now we're here.
We live near a lake called Panic
(Wolves and jackals roam),
We've lived here so long now
It's almost home.
We live near a lake called Panic
(Waters deep as the sea),
Few know it quite as well as
You and me.

Age

Ah! Matt.: old age has brought to me
Thy wisdom, less thy certainty:
The world's a jest, and joy's a trinket:
I knew that once: but now – I think it.

SENEX TO MATT PRIOR
J K STEPHEN (1859–92)

An Apple

Forgive me that from your orchard
I stole an apple or two,

My tree is bare and old,
But yours are green and new.

The First White

Clip clip, she clipped
Behind the left ear,
Clip snip clip,
Above the right temple,
Silver scissors slip scythe-like
Sifting the first sign,
Culling the white wing.

She handed it to me,
A sheaf of sullied corn,
The turncoat hair Judas silver
In a field of full brown.
Here is the harbinger,
O white garment of decay.
Soon your snow-silver
Will cover my head
Like a blanket,
Venerable I may be
In the grey years,
And reconciled with all,
But now I twist in my finger,
In the fine late months of summer,
Slim withered leaves from a full tree,
And feel winter shiver in the blade.

Song of the Old Man

Inside my crumbling house I stand
Which once had seemed the promised land.

And soon this house and all that stood
Must be changed to dust and mud.

The tiles are thin and edged with grey
Windows dim with overlay,

And where the golden flowers were sown
Is cruel with nettles overgrown.

In the cellar chill and rotten
Lie many dreadful things forgotten,
While round each reminiscent room
Memories gather in the gloom.

When I leave this home behind
God only knows what I shall find.

Slumbers in the deepest dark,
Or strolls in some celestial park.

As for eternity to talk and roam,
I think that I shall miss my home.

Suicide Attempt

The room stank of brandy and staleness,
Stale life, stale tears,
And the increasing shadow of tired years
Darkened your room.
This, the first for months.
Was the sleep you fled to and found,
Sleeping the sleep of sleeps,
Broken by breathing.

From each of us
You drew sad breath, sorrow for you,
And we cannot caress
Or reach the walled garden of your self.
By your bed, sad, we sat, waited for you,
Watched your life on the green machine,
The gobbling graph of survival.
Little bundle of flesh, with your mind locked
In sleepiness,
Where are you now?
We cannot call to you
Over the abyss, now and never.
Forget who can the earnest face
Framed by childish plaits?
Ophelia you are, but undrowned.
For round, round you came, yes,
Somewhere in the dark
Life and limb did not part,
And slowly you blinked into the light.
In that light you spoke, hoarse,

Tired with sleeping,
Till we left you to lapse, to lie,
Wallow at the waterhole of dreams.

Then blows fell on your brain,
And you toppled, God knows,
Into the sallow pit of folly
There to remain, lost but alive,
Able-bodied but gentle,
Like a child out of depth in the waking world,
Innocent beyond words, nightmare,
Tossed into jigsaw bits, the mind misted,
All life swimming in that bitter sea
Where every tide pulls this and that
Fragment of deadly wreckage.

And you spoke of what you knew,
(Your sweet-mouthed madness broke and tore us,
Loading us as with a blood-spun wound).

And from each you drew newness,
A seeking into sorrow,
Until your tired startled soul
Shone out a demented flashing beacon,
And your reason reached to find landfall.

Summer's End

Summer's nadir comes, the autumnal clock chimes,
Silly kids slope off to school like migrant birds.
While Keats found autumn splendidly ripe for rhymes
For mortals it's awful autumn-ising words.
After summer's sauna come inclement climes,
From beaches to offices troop herds of nerds,
Great days of the Derby, Wimbledon, Ascot, passed
Like fine grapes on vines too good to last.

How long till the winter reaper raps the door
To jingle my ancient joints with freezing pain?
How long will those dangling fruits endure before
Each lush summer fruit is washed right down the drain?
How long till sleeping oceans wake up with a roar
And short afternoons blow bleakly dark again?
Yes, cry nostalgia for the halcyon weeks
When autumn's breezes start to slap our cheeks!

Years ago, devoid of seasonal care,
Days, weeks, and months passed casual in their turn,
By seventy-five there's not much left to spare
As in old time's frying pan you twist and burn.

(My doctor (young, female), thinks I've had my share
Of summers – it shows she still has much to learn!)

Old Man's Song

This tree will be alive
When I am dead,

These flowers will flare
Vivid red,
Under an opal sky.

Do Not Be Fooled

Do not be fooled
By the middle-aged spread,
The well-fed look,
The embonpoint,
The balding head.

I am the hungry pirate
That I always was,
And on my shoulder sits
A parrot green and red
Riding the ocean swell,
Of the shoulder's peg-leg gait,
Under the lonely moon
'Pieces of eight, pieces of eight,'
Till safe in his cruel beak
I lodge a gold doubloon.

And on the deck
My wooden leg
Drum-like beats out that old tattoo.
I feel a battle coming on
She turns and yardarms ache,
Waves shiver silver
In the brig's wake,

Do not be fooled.

My Eyes are Weaker

Spots and lines, like flies,
Float against the clouds.

Age it is, eyes that have seen too much
Strain at the sky-bright sea,
Or blink bloodshot at the sun.

Curtain

Hearing the audience wheeze and hiss
We never thought our play would end like this,
For after all the passionate verse,
Act Five now goes from bad to worse.

The plot has changed to something strange –
Juliet (whom fair Romeo wed),
Has reached the age of seventy-two instead,
And lovely Romeo, past his prime,
Mopes and frets on prostate time,
Pensive of the moment they will part
Contemplating matters of the heart,
Not poesy but arteries now tax his mind
And does the pulse beat fast or lag behind?

Mercutio, Benvolio, Paris, Tybalt and the rest
Have all gone to another place,
Somewhere downtown, a sweet retiring nest,
Kids grown up, their pensions of the best,
They haven't been seen round here for years
Perhaps some are dead, sick or insane,
Stroked by strange maladies (as one hears),
Nostalgia will not bring them back again.

But what of all the senior lot,
The Capulets and Montagues
Who made the youngsters bold
And reckless till they lost the plot?

Well plots are something that you have to lose,
Sooner or later in the scheme of things,
In time they all lost theirs and gained another,
Parting to eternal dream, the harp, putative
    angelic wings.
Mourned and remembered well,
All sins forgiven, all confessed
And thus all shriven, utterly blessed,
And so (who knows?) they lie in Heaven or Hell.

Now Romeo and Juliet are left alone
Upon a darkening stage.

The audience has gone
And night is coming on.

The Final Chapter and Beyond

Till the sun grows cold,
And the stars are old,
And the leaves of
The Judgement Book unfold.

BEDOUIN SONG
BAYARD TAYLOR (1825–78)

Biddy

I think of her life,
How decisions were difficult for her.
How she clung
To her common sense,
Her universe, her strength,
And never in eighty years
Was anything said
That really changed her mind
About anything.

Right up to death's door
She laughed and rumbled,
And shortly before she finished
She looked suddenly up,
As if puzzled:
"Who are you?
Have I seen you before?
I haven't seen you for years.
Now you stand there
The face is familiar.
What are you doing?"

And the eyes blinked
The lip curled
And she returned to the happy
Blankness of her mind,
Talking about orchards,
And whether she had been
Visited by the dead last week,

And the brothers, and yes,
Her husband lived, and
"I said to him, Cis, what do you think?
And he said, yes!"

And she lived like a child
In the company of the dead,
Living all moments with them,
Smiling at them, knowing them,
Not recognising the living,
But happy with them too
Now there was better company around.

On the morning of the day she died,
When they gave her a bath,
And she looked good and strong,
"Bloody leave me alone!" she said.

And just after that made
Bloody sure they did.

The Passing

He died undisturbed from sea-deep sleep
Inside a silent room put by
For sleepers diagnosed as due to die.

He lay his purple jaws half open,
Eyes purposefully closed,
Almost a smile pinched his nose.

A white sheet primly hid him
As before a shave in a barber's shop,
Almost he casually dozed.
But now how different than when
(A single night before)
His body then still warm,
Yellowed, strangely shrunken,
Changed from that afternoon of
Breathing hard and bitter.
His neck pulse stammered,
Jerked strong but too slowly laboured,
Till a long trough into breath
Dipped undependably the chest's flesh,
Or launched in a gasping crest of movement
Large enough to sustain the beating heart
For a month or more we guessed.
As we watched him struggle there and brood
A blue nozzle plugged his nose,
A feeding pipe taped at one end to his brow,
Hair uncombed, familiar silver,
His mouth propped open with a rubber wedge.

Perhaps he might open his eyes
Suddenly to find us there (we thought)
Staring at him for the leave-taking.

The Scattering

(In Memoriam Jack Fowles)

I can't quite take my mind off
that white bag
our host had placed and hidden
like gold dust in the car,
till extracted from its cardboard box
like a conjuring trick
it attracted the eye.

But first he brought out
paper cups and a bottle,
and said how his dear father, Jack,
"was lucky as well as brave",
and now we stood,
as it were, by an open grave.

We had searched through swelling rain
for this place, under the mountain's clouded crag,
among desolate barracks, fields, hangars,
a broken control tower, a dome where gunners had
    trained.

Having drained the cup,
time to bid farewell,
and gathering like boys,
invited to take good handfuls each,
we thrust with naked fingers,
sinking the wrist in thick ash,
as if grasping sand,
and with filled hand carefully,

tossed crisp powder to the wind,
over the long grass,
somewhere near where
Jack (sixty years before) flew his plane
to survive accident and loss.
And when wet green bloomed like blossom, white
   with ash,
and scatterings ceased after many returns,
hands refilling, re-spilling gentle soil to earth,
the white bag emptied to its last speck,
the sun that instant peeled the skin of clouds off hills,
and shone on the faded camouflage of hut and tower,
with no more overcast.

As we drove off,
faces moist, shy handkerchiefs dabbed,
along the rutted path that leads away,
a cat, its black coat reflecting light,
slipped into thorn and bush.

We watched its going
with the hush that comes as in a church,
when the sad service is over, the worst is past.

And, as if reprieved, each
accepts the silent moment
for what it's worth.

Anna

Her slow dying
Gives pause for thought.

Eagerly she suckles soup,
Thin fingers at the beaker's edge,
Fingers which once teased out
A Chopin *Nocturne* easily
Like tickling trout.

And when I help
She puts her warm palm
Gently, as in love,
Upon my arm.

Watching, I think
Of billions dying so
In damp battlefields of beds,
Or some lost sailor
Aching
After days of swimming,
Sighting a distant breaking shore,
Who can give no more,
Swim no more,
Do no more.

No more.

Song of the Very Old Man

"Everybody's gone,
Everything we had to say,
Is said."

He sits under a sickly sky,
By a whispering sea

Thinking of the dead.

After a Funeral

I return
As if from a distant place.

A low sun
Touches the sea,
Blue smooth light.

Waves like widows weep
But I'll not go back there.

John

Street friend (the place we always met),
just minutes,
long enough for,
life sketches,
travails registered,
tales of medical maladministrations,
nursely indelicacies,
aneurisms, life scars.

And you, with your slow walk,
dragging bags of vegetables,
from town,
wire-rimmed spectacles,
ailments by list, by rote.

Christmas cards
thrust into your empty house,
returned by lawyers,
"Regret to say...etc."

The street is bare,
no more your sickness.

So there we have it
and no more.

Forethought

Soon we shall go,
And never see each other.

Love's memory
Will hang in the sunset
Like a spider's web.

Accept

We accept
The tide will out.

Till then
Play on the beach,

Look at the sea,
Absorb the sky.

In Memoriam

(Susan McGowan's suicide)

At one savage point
In time's flow,
What we had said at length
Together, in congenial evening talk,
She forgot.

She who believed in spirits,
Not in accustomed things,
Has forsaken the spirit of life.

Her death is
Our conscience now.

The unwritten letters squeal
From the mind's pigeon-hole.
I remember a shabby delay
Not long ago
To answer what seems now
A call.

Her words typed
On the scented page
Assume a levity she
Seldom let fall, yet
There it is all written
For those who had eyes to see.

Leaves

Stepping on dead leaves
Reminds me of the dead.

Their outflung forms,
Their lostness,
The battlefield colour
Their colour.

So flat and trodden,
Flung and forgotten
From the tree of life.

In a Crematorium Garden

In scattered ash
No recall
Of dawns or violet sunsets.

No longer to laugh at folly
Or mourn memories of love.

Only the sinister whispering of the grass,
Particles of the past,

Tinglings of time,
Nothing to last.

After She Died

Where are you, sun?
Why this particular night
Do you have to drag your golden feet so slowly?

And when the dawn came up
It was dirty grey,
With a blotched touch of blood
Over the mourning sea.

Revelation

Each Sabbath I said the words,
Believing in the Resurrection of the Dead.

Now no longer can that be true
Whatever words are said.

She lies in ashes, lost and mourned,
Like Wordsworth's girl rolled round and round,
Scattered on the weed-strewn ground.

One day we will be burned by the sun,
All prophecies fulfilled – save one.

Three Short Stories

Gethsemane

How many stars could be counted on a night like this? He started counting, mouthing the numbers under his breath, counting slowly. When he arrived at two thousand he stopped counting.

His knees on the parched earth pained him. The night's coldness was bitter, a cold extenuated by the harsh light of stars. He lifted up his face once more to that uninhabited emptiness. A bead of sweat rolled its way along the ridge of his nose. Licking his lips, the salt tang of his saliva, reminded him of his body, deflected his thoughts from the horror of space.

Nevertheless he forced himself to name each planet, each constellation. The navigators, the sailors, the fishermen – they used the infinite spaces of the heavens for their daily toil. He escaped again from his body's weight, that tiredness. The moon was full, gleaming, deathly.

A loud snore pulled him back to earth. They were sleeping then, after all his warnings. Stretched out, wrapped in cloaks of many colours, their faces as white as corpses with cold, fear, and the moon. The brightness lit up the hills, shrubs, the twisted olives, malformed stone. More snores, the sleepy grunts of men in bad sleep.

He sighed to himself, the sound coming from the corner of his mouth, the breath expelled from the lungs into a low moan. He wiped a finger across his brow and placed the moist tip onto his tongue. He licked it deliberately, slowly, savouring the rasp of roughness on lips, the tinge of bitterness.

He thought back over the history of his race. Their brooding for centuries under these stars, the slow fighting over the land from the point of man's beginning. Here, in this time, minute by minute, was the culmination. After tonight the perspectives would change.

He felt dizzy with the magnitude of his thoughts and the scope of that sky. One of them cried out in his sleep and the legs thrashed against the hard yellow soil. They were not capable, after all, of understanding. Small wonder. Rooted in the physical life around them, they were nature's weaklings, human, weak, lacking as yet, inner resources. On their frail bodies the foundation would rest, all the same, the whole edifice. Strength would come later.

In this moment, on this night, their weakness touched him. A shooting star spat across the heavens. Its brilliance was such, he felt he could reach and pull it to earth, snap it in a closed fist, drag it within reach, its movement inexorable, violent, like the movement of a plane on a shaft of wood.

A line of music touched his mind. The monody of a beggar, blind from birth, seen a few days before, trotting aimlessly for ever towards no destination; a dribble of saliva and froth masking his jowls in cuckoo-pint. He had no arms. The stumps moved backwards and forwards like the wings of a bird as he walked, keeping his balance. Still a snatch of song.

He put his open palm against this face. Despite the chill he was running a temperature, the ferment rising in the top of the skull to lose itself in perspiration. This garden was a frightful place. Sometimes at night soldiers roamed here with women. They clambered over the walls, clattering against stones and bush, then into the trivial cover of hedges. Other men came too, full of the flesh, unaware of the night, stars, or time itself. After the fit was over they were satiated and went, jocular or morbid, back to the familiar lights of barracks or home.

But tonight not one came. He knew. Tonight the garden was unmolested. The sleeping showed their exhaustion. They trusted his presence as children trust their parents even if danger is near. Normally the garden's reputation was notorious, a place to avoid at night. Tonight the empty serenity of stars infiltrated the slopes and shrubs which gave shelter.

He felt a movement against the back of his hand, extending down towards the wrist. Gently he brought his arm flat in front of him. A small creature was crawling, painstakingly, picking its way along the ridges and hairs of his arm. He watched its progress. A speck on holy flesh. Wat it aware? A difficult philosophical issue, even for the Pharisees;

'If you are the Son of God, make that insect acknowledge you. Surely we can expect no less.'

'Which is more difficulty, I ask you?' To make a man acknowledge that I am the Son of God, or this lowly insect?"

That could not be answered. If they chose an insect, the Pharisees would look ridiculous in the eyes of the blind who had been healed. To say anything else would reflect on their own lack of belief. Their dark faces were haunted with despair. When men become confused with their labyrinth of logic, they move forward into violence, force, murder.

Tonight his body troubled him with the anxiety of the coming of death. He tried to avoid too great a concentration on its physical details, trying to see beyond as one might try to see behind the stars, into the blackness which soon would be smashed by the sun's light.

The insect advanced, faltered, moved again. He spoke to it, breathed on it, its wings responding and vibrating to the light pressure of his speaking. Then it flew off his arm into the dark, lost for ever but alive.

He began his prayers, throwing up his thoughts to the immensity, the giant processes of the energy bringing again heat to his face and body. The back of his arm burned like fire.

And

I had stayed with the Yamuri tribe for a matter of some months. The oppressive watery heat of the hottest season had already started. As research graduate in anthropological semantics I looked forward to the assignment with pleasure, despite the fact that certain authorities in this field (including, I am sorry to say, my own professor) believed that the Yamuris offered little in the way of interesting or original material.

For one thing there were not many of them. Their natural habitat in the crook of a minor tributary of the Amazon had made them highly vulnerable to the incursions of the white man. By the time I arrived at their settlement fewer than forty or fifty of the Yamuri remained in their pure unspoiled state and several of these were not particularly healthy. Having read *The Last of the Mohicans* when I was a boy, the tragic dilemma in which the Yamuris now found themselves had in it some aspects of familiarity.

About their ultimate survival there was little or nothing I could do. So after a few days of acclimatisation, and suitably accommodated in one of the huts where the Yamuri tribesman could maintain some measure of relative comfort, I started work. From the outset it became clear that their language was quite distinct from the tribal dialects of Indians even a few miles away. It was undoubtedly an unusual language, hampered naturally by its lack of any literacy and yet preserving a purity of outline and grammatical usage entirely appropriate to itself.

Most of the words in the Yamuri language were of one syllable in length. There existed no word for 'I' or any personal possessive such as 'my' or 'mine' or even 'our' or 'ours'. In the tribal context of their lives this lack of the first person pronoun certainly contained its own kind of logic. All things, from tobacco to wives, from quinine leaf to arrows, being shared, the Yamuri had no need for the immediate linguistic indications of personal identity. One felt that the mere invention of such a word would have occasioned a kind of psychic revolution from which each and every Yamuri would never have recovered.

However, the language possessed other peculiarities, subtle refinements, which from the first puzzled the training and instinct of any semanticist, even one versed in anthropological and primitive linguistic patterns. For example the word for 'bird' was a guttural sound which can best be transcribed as *grerrg*; the word for 'leaf' was *tarrgh*. But the equivalent of our conjunction 'and' (which was extraordinarily often used and never in a shortened form) seemed to be the only word in their language of more than one syllable. This word can be transliterated as *yahghschnasssrahgh*.

Thus one could often encounter such a surprising sentence of *grerrg yahghschnasssrahgh tarrgh* for the phrase 'bird and leaf', a statement in which the conjunction assumed a higher degree of significance within the phrase than the principal words themselves. (Unfortunately it is impossible to indicate within European transliteration of Yamuri either those exquisite tonal inflections of each syllable or their expressive guttural onomatopoeia which gave to their utterance a refreshing spontaneity, hence the purity of diction to which I have already referred).

The only logical explanation of the development of this weighty conjunction could be that things lumped together assume a higher significance. Thus the conjunction 'and' became elevated to the level of real expressive importance, a concept not at all amenable to European linguistics where in each instance the conjunction is the smallest, least forceful of any part of speech (even allowing for deliberate stressing on the part of the speaker).

I also discovered during the course of my stay that the Yamuri seemed to take a special delight in their conjunction as some means of imparting to the monosyllabic language an extra polyrhythmic refinement, a kind of tongue-twisting virtuosity adding to the technical variety of their speech.

It was not uncommon to hear quite tiny children repeating the word endlessly, much as a European infant might delight in mouthing nursery rhymes. Against the swishing of the river, the occasional squawking of tame parrots, and assorted forest and village noises, the childish repetition of *yahghschnasssrahgh*, *yahghschnasssrahgh*, presented a delightful counterpoint.

The toddlers played with the syllables on the tongue, repeated them, rolled them back and forward like an incantation or a trick of memorising, whispered or shouted, growled or sung, prolonging or shortening each syllable and sound, and subjecting the word to an almost symphonic process of variation. After an hour or two of listening to this I found the voices stuck in memory like a phrase of music infinitely refined, repeated till it became part of the beat of one's own pulse.

In my diary, damp with the heat and slightly stained with Indian tobacco juice, I wrote a few observations about these doomed children. '*Not too many years from now the sounds of these tiny fluting voices may be as extinct as the rarest of some primeval bird whose existence has only been guessed at. Even those who survive will succumb to the incessant tide of the white man's language.*'

As the days and weeks gently passed it seemed that the Yamuri noticed my presence less and less. They could not exactly forget that I was there as my grasp of their language had not yet acquired the fluency essential for complete understanding.

They still treated me, as always, with the utmost kindness and the women unfailingly prepared food for me, grinding and beating the roots into a fine flour-like powder and fetching fruit from the forest. But a strange sensation of their growing apathy, amounting to a fatalistic indifference, permeated even the essential acts of kindness.

Ta kou jjamm grerrg jjamm! explained one of the young men, smoking a long slender pipe, his intoxication reflected in the mildly blood-shot cast of his left eye; *yahghschnasssrahgh jjamm kou traghgh.* In my diary I roughly translated this (although its subtlety cannot fully be rendered in translation) as *The limed bird is trapped and we share its predicament.* To this I replied with the formal Yamuri retort (though inadequately, as the Yamuri tongue is impervious to accurate pronunciation by a European), *Ganghgh chrughgh slan kou, (Long may fate linger before dark falls).*

My camera, tape-recorder and books were stored next to my camp-bed in the hut the senior men of the village had built for me. Inside was relatively cool as Yamuri architecture, curiously evolved, allowed the air to circulate under the hut itself, the structure being mounted on small stilts, as an additional safeguard against flooding or subsidence. (The only disadvantage of their method of construction being that small rodents, insects, waste matter and stagnant water tended to collect under the floor of the hut in certain seasons).

The Yamuri never entered my hut or even looked inside, but often in the early morning they congregated outside for some reason, pausing to chatter among themselves in speculative terms. For example, dreams fascinated them and through the thin walls of the hut I could often hear them enquiring among themselves of how many dreams or nightmares had been experienced during the hours of sleep. (Their word for sleep *terrrmgh* even now falls on my ears with delicious somnolent softness).

One morning, a little after sunrise, arising from a particularly heavy *terrrmgh* induced by an excess of smoking the Yamuri's favourite leaf (which they invariably insisted on sharing with me despite its comparative rarity in this part of the forest), I became aware of activity outside my quarters. I lay still and switched on the tape-recorder hoping to capture some of the little confidences and comments. After the traditional morning salutations and a few shared dreams I heard it announced that this was to be the day of the ritual (an extended hunt far into the forest), undertaken only once every few years by all the men and boys of the Yamuri.

To my considerable disappointment I also understood that only full-blooded Yamuri tribesmen would undertake the *niergghgh* and I would remain behind with the women. Only initiates of the tribe (a ceremony on the male side which took place soon after birth, rather like the Jewish rites of circumcision) were permitted to walk the sacred groves of the deep forest beyond the two river crossings. Even boys of a tender age were expected to take part in the expedition.

Anthropologically the *niergghgh* dated back in all probability to pre-Conquistadores eras when this part of the forest was entirely inhabited by the Yamuri and before off-shoots of the tribe were absorbed by marriage and migration into the human mixture of less pure-blooded Indians. Only thus could the leaving behind of the women and girls be satisfactorily accounted for.

I roused myself gently, feeling a little dizzy, and slowly dressed. On emerging from the privacy of my hut into the bright light of the compound I noticed that the Yamuri wore a type of war-paint I had not seen before.

Ta kou jjamm grerrg jjamm! said the same young man I had spoken to the day before, a sly grin playing around the corners of his painted mouth.

Ganghgh chrughgh, I replied and quickly added, *yahghschnasssrahgh grahggh niergghgh kinnm yagh* (meaning of course 'May the hunting meet with success as you deserve'). On this occasion my formal words were met with a peal of laughter from men and women alike, and they gathered round, breathing on me as a sign of friendship, slapping me heartily on the back, and ever so gently mocking my clumsy mispronunciation of their precious language (especially in the case of the conjunction with its double-gutturals and omnitones).

This show of friendship amazed me, for nothing even remotely like it had occurred previously. But then, I reflected, the traditional *niergghgh* was very special, rather like Christmas to them, and even more special that its advent was kept an almost total secret till the day dawned.

The hunters played a few games with the women before departing, chasing the young virgins into the bushes and round the trees, throwing a bucket of dirty water over one of the dogs, slapping the bare backsides of the older women, and enacting a small ritual dance, tapping rhythmically with their spears on the ground, before beginning to wend their way down this well-trodden path south along the river bank. The women, after indulging gleefully in the horseplay, watched them depart (a little sadly I thought), before returning to their huts and the daily chores.

As the sun grew hotter a strange silence came over the village broken only by the usual river sounds, an occasion barking dog, and the never-ending forest noises.

So we waited for the men's return. I doodled a little with the dictionary I had begun to form of everyday Yamuri vocabulary, uncertain as always of the exact transliteration of various words. I listened to the tape-recordings of their language over and over again, a game which never particularly interested the women once the novelty had worn off.

We waited three days, five days, eight days, and then two more days. The women carried on with their normal activities, planting, sowing, pounding roots, gathering fruit, killing pigs, trapping birds. One of the dogs had puppies. Some of the words for my dictionary became less intractable; other seemed more difficult than ever.

After twelve days the women became suddenly morose. No one would tell me how long the hunt would last. One of the oldest members of the tribe, a great-grandmother or *prieggh*, died unexpectedly one afternoon though she had been quite active in the morning. With little outward signs of distress or mourning the women took her body off on a bamboo stretcher to their secret burial mounds.

On the fourteenth day two or three of the younger women became ill and on the eighteenth day the entire village population of twenty-seven Yamuri women seemed in the grip of a fatal languor. On the twentieth day I too went down with a strange fever which took a day or two to deal with and most of my supply of quinine.

By the thirtieth day six or seven more women (of various ages), and two babies had died. But the men still did not return.

On the thirty-fifth day since the *niergghgh* began I was woken shortly after dawn by an incessant moaning. I dragged myself out of bed and moved into the bright dazzle of the compound.

There on the ground, an ugly bullet-wound in his upper leg, lay a young man. As I bent over him he spoke in a pained whisper, *Ta kou jjamm.* A trickle of blood oozed from the corner of his mouth. I noticed purple bruising on his arms, chest and face as if he had been beaten with some heavy club or rifle butt. His war-paint was gone.

The women, those still able to walk and move about, carried him into my hut and laid him on the camp-bed. In a matter of minutes be became mildly delirious and repeated endlessly some form of the Yamuri language I had not heard before. (Fortunately I managed to switch on the tape-recorder next to the bed and preserve for posterity some of this strange guttural sound. On close listening you can distinctly make out the word *niergghgh* and also *tranggh* meaning death, destruction or catastrophe). I left the hut for a breath of air while the women gently moaned and ministered to him.

Shortly before he died some hours later, the women summoned me to his bedside. He was no longer delirious but in considerable pain. The women had dressed his wound with leaves and given him some of the forest herbs to ease his agony.

Strangely trusting and child-like he looked at me full in the face and with a tiny anguished smile muttered quite comprehensibly, *Ta kou jjamm*. He reached out his hand and touched my arm.

Before he died, this, the last male of the Yamuri, pronouncing his benediction, and as if to give me a memory of his tribe's suffering, gently whispered *Yahghschnasssrahgh… yahghschnasss… yahgh…*.

The Golden Guitar of the Pharaoh's Daughter

In the 1950s, I worked as a young man in the Egyptology section of the British Museum. At the time, there was much talk of the survival (somewhere in Egypt) of a golden guitar, the beloved toy of a Pharaoh's daughter. As I had recently begun to play the guitar, such speculation fed my imagination like a furnace.

In terms of accuracy this Egyptian instrument must have been a lute, or something similar, not really a guitar, just a plucked chordophone. But we didn't bother much then with exactitude. I wanted to think of the object as a guitar and persuaded my boss along the same lines. We even had people from Cairo saying they had seen one or two such 'guitars' in archaeological sites and museums and perhaps we ought to acquire one. I became so excited that not only was my head crammed with endless notions but I also became the laughing stock of the department.

Eventually I was considered so tiresome that my boss chose (for reasons of his own sanity), to send me to the land of the Pyramids to see if such a treasure could be found. When I stepped on that ship in London docks bound for Port Said, it was the happiest day of my life.

Egypt was not what I thought it was going to be. The food was lethal, the heat intolerable, and the museums and diggings inexhaustible (unlike myself). I tried to enthuse my colleagues with my own spirit of dream, describing the mythical instrument in exaggerated detail, praising its uniqueness, its beauty, and desirability. Some seemed persuaded, others laughed, one patient man took me to a Cairo museum to show me a statue of a girl playing almost the kind of instrument I had envisaged. So such a thing had existed – all we needed was to find the extant original.

Unfortunately, as ever, fate took a hand (not perhaps the Pharaoh's curse falling on tomb pillagers but something almost as bad). I plunged into a feverish condition and was confined to bed, the doctors ordering my return to London as soon as possible.

The fever deepened. I was never sure where I was or even in which country. One night I awoke from troubled sleep and through the mosquito net saw a beautiful young woman, scantily clad, playing a small guitar. I didn't have my spectacles on but it was apparently a gold guitar, ornate with jewels. From her slim fingertips came the most extraordinary ethereal sound. I had never heard such tone, such ecstasy drawn from plucked strings.

When the exquisite melody subsided with a chord, she placed the instrument on a chair, came towards me and lifted up the mosquito net. She laid her soft lips on mine in a passionate kiss. Unable, in my weakness, to resist or proceed, I fell back on the pillow. I must have swooned with debility and joy, for when I awoke I was alone again.

In the morning I pondered why such a dream seemed so real. I still imagined the pressure of her lips and the aftersound of the melody. Bemused, I searched the room and found a little pearl ear-ring on the floor where the apparition had stood. Did it belong to the Princess? Or to the cleaning maid?

When well enough to go to communal breakfast in the hotel, I told my colleagues about the dream, the guitar, its adornments, the girl, the mosquito net, the kiss. I even triumphantly brought out the ear-ring. They laughed a lot and looked at each other in conspiratorial jokiness, wishing that they too could catch the same deadly virus.

'But it was so real!' I said.

'More like surreal!' muttered one of the more unpleasant professors, producing his own tidal wave of guffaws, hilarity, titters and ridicule. 'The sooner you get back on that boat, the better. We don't want Pharaoh visiting one night for punishment after you interfered with his daughter! And you'd better send the ear-ring back, care of the Pyramids!'

'Malaria, old boy!' said another.

My fever seemed to be returning but I laughed with them at the folly of dreams, putting the ear-ring in my wallet as a memento of paradise. Over the years I told this story at dinner parties round the world, developing it to suit particular companions. Medical types received more emphasis on malarial delusion, at which they nodded sagely. For guitarists I gave more scope to the description of the instrument. For coarser audiences (lawyers, accountants, business-men), I concentrated on the girl's magnetism, the allure of her body and perfume, etc., spinning the web spider-like to draw them in. Finally I flourished the ear-ring like a conjuror. Sometimes I might be invited to repeat the story for new guests and I was most pleased to oblige.

Most of the dreams of youth have now been discarded on the journey. In my twenties I married the girl of my dreams who later became my nightmare. I have seen much of society move from romantic meditation in quiet houses with books, hobbies, radio and conversation to something entirely different. Today's guitar heroes are multi-millionaire rock artists whose music nauseates me. My own heroes have mainly departed the battlefield though by no means all of them. Were these dreams within dreams, hopes within hopes, mere delusions once cherished, like the vision of the Pharaoh's daughter? Or were such dreams of music and poetry the secret thread of gold which the world has momentarily lost?

However, quite by chance, I did receive an answer to the problem of the Pharaoh's daughter. At a Boxing Day dinner party to which I was introduced last year by one of my most respected friends, once again, like a well-trained (though slightly inebriated) circus animal, I embarked on my perennial party trick.

After I had finished my perhaps too finely rehearsed narrative and, with a twirl of the hand, offered the ear-ring round for inspection, our hostess, a total stranger till that night, looked closely at the trinket, and then at her husband. His face, and hers, suddenly turned quite pale.

I thought I had committed some social faux pas and spluttered an apology. The woman looked up at me, placing the ear-ring on the table cloth. She was slightly older than myself, a definite but faded beauty in her face - a dark complexion, brown eyes, almost oriental eyebrows.

'I am very sorry,' she said. 'It is I who must apologise.'

We waited for whatever followed.

'You did not dream!' she whispered. 'Your Cairo colleagues persuaded me to perform that night. My mother was Egyptian, my father a British consul, and I was young and foolish. I put on fancy dress and decided to round the evening off for you. That's when you touched my hair, the clasp became loose and the ear-ring was dropped.'

The guests shook their heads. I could scarcely breathe. With that she handed back the ear-ring, and with it another, its double.

'And the music you played?'

'That was a little recording from outside the door. I can't play an instrument myself, I never could (though I can dance). We decorated a little guitar with gold paper and mock jewels.'

'There!' exclaimed my friend with glee. 'Next time you tell the story you can give it an ending.'

It took me some weeks to recover from this revelation. The borders between dream and memory were restored. But it led to other questions.

Were all our young dreams illusions, self-deception, folly? Was even art itself – the accumulated offerings of great artists, all the music, literature and artefacts of centuries piled up in museums like so much detritus – nothing but a kind of fevered dream?

The hostess insisted I keep both ear-rings. She looked at me meaningfully as I left, as if old acquaintances had at last been reunited.

But I didn't quite feel that way. If anything I felt rather let down, as if something irretrievably precious had been lost.

I have not been to any dinner parties since. But, either way, I don't want to tell that story again. Like a lot of things, the picture has changed.

Now nothing, not even the memory of a dream, will ever seem quite the same.

Acknowledgments

Various poems in this collection appeared in the following publications:

The Literary Review, The Arts Council of Britain (New Poetry), Creative Guitar International, Classical Guitar, The Sunday Times, Poetry Now, Old Persean magazine, Echoes from Within.

I would like to thank John Carrington for his in-depth *Foreword* to this book and long time friend Brian Swann, for *Winkie.*

I would like to acknowledge the inestimable help in the production of this publication by Miles Bailey, John Chandler and Vivian Hawkins. Thanks also to Mareth Fielding for typing assistance with the manuscript.

As always I must express my profound gratitude to my wife, Sue, for her patience and guidance during the compilation of these poems.

Also by Graham Wade

Biographical Studies

Profile of Federico Mompou (Naxos ebook, 2011)

Profile of Joaquín Turina (Naxos ebook, 2011)

Profile of Manuel de Falla (Naxos ebook, 2011)

Nombres Propios de la Guitarra: Julian Bream
(Córdoba Lecture, IMAE Gran Teatro &
Ayuntamiento de Córdoba, 2009)

The Art of Julian Bream (Ashley Mark, 2008)

Portrait of Rodrigo, His Life, His Music
(Naxos, 2008, with 86 page booklet by Graham Wade)

Francisco Tárrega (1852–1909)
(Stanley Yates & Graham Wade, Mel Bay, DVD, 2008)

Joaquín Rodrigo – A Life in Music (GRM Publications, 2006)

Gina Bachauer – A Pianist's Odyssey (GRM Publications, 1999)

John Mills, Concert Guitarist – A Celebration
(GRM Publications, 1997)

A New Look at Segovia, His Life, His Music, Vols 1 & 2
(with Gerard Garno, Mel Bay, 1996)

Maestro Segovia (Robson, 1986)

Segovia – a Celebration of the Man and his Music
(Allison & Busby, 1983)

Classical Guitar Publications

Traditions of the Classical Guitar
(All World Classics, re-print from 1980 edition, 2012)

Classical Guitar – A Complete History (ed. John Morrish, thirteen
essays by Graham Wade, Balafon, 2002)

Distant Sarabandes – The Solo Guitar Music of Joaquín Rodrigo
(GRM Publications, 2nd Edition 2001)

A Concise History of the Classic Guitar (Mel Bay, 2001)

Guitar Teaching and Learning – Interpretation and Style
(University of Reading, 1998)

The Guitarist's Guide to Associated Board Examinations
(Graham Wade and Brian Jeffery, GRM Publications
& Tecla Editions, 1997)

The Guitarist's Guide to J.S. Bach (Wise Owl Music, 1985)

Joaquín Rodrigo – Concierto de Aranjuez (Mayflower Press, 1985)

Your Book of the Guitar (Faber 1980)

Graham Wade/ICS Guitar Course, Vols I & II
(International Correspondence Schools, 1972 & 1975)

GENERAL MUSIC PUBLICATIONS

A Concise Guide to Understanding Music (Mel Bay, 2003)

The Shape of Music (Allison & Busby, 1983)

NOVELS

The Emperor's Barber (The Choir Press, 2017)

The Fibonacci Confessions
(GRM Publications 2010, The Choir Press, re-published 2017)

POEMS

Aranjuez and Other Poems (In Remembrance of Joaquín Rodrigo)
(GRM Publications, 2016)

Goats in the Trees (and other Moroccan Poems),
(GRM Publications, 2015)

Daniel and the Lions (A performance poem for young people)
(GRM Publications, 2015)

Mother and Other Poems (GRM Publications, 2001)

Frog and Other Poems (GRM Publications, 2001)

War Baby and Other Poems (GRM Publications, 2000)

In Whim or Design (Denstone College, 1969)

TRANSLATIONS

Heitor Villa-Lobos and the Guitar, Turibio Santos (Translated and
edited by Victoria Forde & Graham Wade, Wise Owl, 1985)

EDITIONS: EDITED BY ELIZABETH AND GRAHAM
WADE,
MEL BAY PAPERBACK SERIES

A Concise History of the Electric Guitar, Adrian Ingram
(Mel Bay, 2001)

A Concise Guide to Musical Terms, John Robert Brown
(Mel Bay, 2002)

A Concise History of Jazz, John Robert Brown (Mel Bay, 2004)

A Concise History of Rock, Paul Fowles (Mel Bay, 2009)

A Concise History of 20th Century Music, Graham Hearn
(Mel Bay, 2010)

A Concise Guide to Orchestral Music, 1700 to the Present Day,
David Fligg (Mel Bay, 2010)

Reviews and Comments

Traditions of the Classical Guitar

Graham Wade has shown his love of the guitar from the first page to the last – true love and understanding. ANDRÉS SEGOVIA

The most important recent publication of the last few years...The first stylistic critique of guitar music from the beginning through all the centuries. JÜRGEN LIBBERT, NEUE MUSIKZEITSCHRIFT

Segovia – A Celebration of the Man and His Music

Graham Wade has spent a generous amount of time putting together this book in praise of 'my first' 90 years. My gratitude corresponds faithfully to his noble intention and the arduous work accomplished...I hope that this lively and affectionate book will be received with the appreciation and success it merits. ANDRÉS SEGOVIA

A New Look at Segovia, His Life, His Music, Volumes 1 & 2 (with Gerard Garno)

The most remarkable piece of classical guitar scholarship we are ever likely to see. BRENDAN McCORMACK, INTERNATIONAL GUITAR FESTIVAL OF GREAT BRITAIN

Gina Bachauer – A Pianist's Odyssey

I treasure every page of this fascinating biography, a beautiful testimony of love and admiration of both the human being as well as the artist who has left us with so much to enrich our lives. IRENE, PRINCESS OF GREECE

This book provides an excellent record of a unique life. SIR EDWARD HEATH

I know of no biography of any pianist – not even the greatest in the world – whose life, both musical and personal, has been chronicled in such illuminating detail. No music lover in the world could fail to enjoy every page of this vivid story. JOAN CHISSELL

The Art of Julian Bream

Graham Wade is the ideal writer to undertake the task of writing a detailed book about the musical achievements of our most celebrated guitarist...This book is surely indispensable to anyone who values the work of Julian Bream...It comes off successfully, even triumphantly, and will be the definitive book on Julian Bream for a long time to come.

COLIN COOPER, CLASSICAL GUITAR

This eminently readable and quite fascinating book, superbly and generously illustrated, is most enthusiastically recommended.

ROBERT MATTHEW-WALKER,
INTERNATIONAL RECORD REVIEW

Joaquín Rodrigo – A Life in Music
(Travelling to Aranjuez 1901–1939)

My family and I believe that this is the book which needed to be written and that it will generate an enormous interest in both the music and the life of Joaquín Rodrigo.   CECILIA RODRIGO,
MARQUESA DE LOS JARDINES DE ARANJUEZ

Author Graham Wade has become the composer's Boswell...Rodrigo's fascinating life story comes shining through...the Rodrigo lover's jackpot.
PHILIP CLARK, BOOK OF THE MONTH, CLASSIC FM MAGAZINE

This first biography of Rodrigo in English is further testament to Graham Wade's seemingly inexhaustible energies...a terrific tale...a revelatory read.   ANDREW GREEN, CLASSICAL MUSIC

Enter the tireless author, teacher and guitarist, Graham Wade, to tell a story of even more tireless determination to succeed. And the music in all its unfamiliar range is the heart of Wade's mammoth undertaking, the first in English.   ROBERT MAYCOCK, BBC MUSIC

The Shape of Music

I know of no book like this on the subject of music: and apart from the wealth of information which it contains, it is every bit as absorbing as a work of popular general literature on any subject.

MALCOLM WILLIAMSON,
MASTER OF THE QUEEN'S MUSIC

Mother and Other Poems

Graham Wade's best are his tragic poems, which is rare for most incitements to pity by modern verse-writers are mere sentimentality...His poems have the true pathos of the soul.   KATHLEEN RAINE

The Fibonacci Confessions

It reads as if it could be a movie, fast, moving, exotic, lots of adventure – I really enjoyed everything I read, particularly the tenth letter, through the wilderness with Guillaume, and the sixth letter too in Egypt. Congratulations!
PROFESSOR BRIAN SWANN
(DEPARTMENT OF LITERATURE, COOPER UNION, NEW YORK)

This is an excellent book I would recommend to anyone. I was particularly struck by the form of your presentation of a twisting and turning story in letter form to re-create the life of Leonardo not only in his own words, but those of others closely involved in the plot as well... I envy you in completing every writer's dream!
CHARLES POSTELWATE (GRANBURY, TEXAS)

A huge achievement. Impressively written – stylish, assured, beautifully structured, not a word out of place. Very satisfying (and easy) to read. Triumphant prose. Wholly convincing in its exotic period flavour, elegant and sharply detailed. Poetic and sensuous.
Many congratulations on what is undoubtedly a stupendous achievement – it must be very fulfilling for you that the novel is born, after a gestation of fifteen years.
My abiding memory is that I have very much enjoyed the rich panorama, wonderfully detailed and evoked, of so many aspects of life in the 12TH/13TH Century, the unfolding excitement of the mathematical quest, the voyages, and the company of the enigmatic hero!
JOHN CARRINGTON (TAUNTON, DEVON)

Marvellous book. I congratulate you. You are obviously a master of the language. What impressed me was your ability to capture a style that seems of the period and yet you didn't revert to tricks in trying to imitate the language of the twelfth century. You did a wonderful job. It was fascinating.
PATRICK READ (SAN FRANCISCO)

I want to congratulate you for your fantastic research and for your fantasy. I didn't know that on top of guitarist, scholar, writer, and more, you are also a mathematician!   CECILIA RODRIGO (MADRID)

This is an amazing book. You are drawn in and the characters are clearly visible. The writing is sumptuous and engulfs you in a richly embroidered Renaissance cloak.

BRIAN JERVIS (GERMANY)

The Emperor's Barber

A fascinating, entertaining, and strange tale of how a lowly Turkish orphan rises up to become one of the most influential noblemen in the court of Emperor Paul I of Russia. Award-winning author Graham Wade has turned out yet another gem, giving his readers a peek into the history of possibly the nadir of the Russian Empire.

CHARLES POSTELWATE (GRANBURY, TEXAS)

A riveting story of adventure, romance, and retribution, this beautifully crafted historical novel by Graham Wade recounts the meteoric rise of an orphaned peasant boy from Turkey to the exalted position of confidant to the Emperor of Russia, the insane son of Catherine the Great.

CHRIS DELL (ENGLAND, UK)

I encountered in The Emperor's Barber a fascinating character, strikingly similar to the hero of The Fibonacci Confessions, a wanderer of ambivalent and obscure origins, a resourceful opportunist totally devoid of moral considerations, courageous, exceptionally clever, devious and malign. A man who serves only himself and whose deference (often sycophantic) to others, while devoid of sincerity is simulated with devilish conviction. Kutaissov verges on caricature at times. He also exercises a kind of Mephistophelian fascination on the reader –like Shakespeare's Richard of Gloucester and Iago, or like Dickens's Quilp….

NICHOLAS BLYTH (ENGLAND, UK)